Surviving Family Care Giving

*Care Giving: Co-ordinating effective care
...ve communication* is a practical book for
...home carers in a variety of situations. Gráinne
...now to provide the most effective co-ordinated care
...ough constructive communication and collaborative
...pport individuals who have long-term physical and
...alth problems including conditions from Alzheimer's
...ism, autism to anorexia, schizophrenia to multiple

...en from personal experience as a family carer, Gráinne
...ludes interviews with other carers and service users
...s on years of working with children and their families
...gh times. Chapters such as Challenging Behaviour,
...lity, and Motivation illustrate some of the many
...acing carers who support vulnerable individuals.
...include isolation, feelings of helplessness and
...about what is best to do, what to try to avoid, and
...much-needed relevant information and resources to
...re giving.

...ing Family Care Giving vividly illustrates the daily
...s experienced by care givers who offer long-term care
...rt – and shows how to work through them. It provides
...ns for ways to build both constructive collaborative
...good family teamwork through effective communi-
...nd how to ensure continuing care and support for the
...t the centre of all the efforts. This book will be essential
reading for family and other carers, including professionals
trying to create ongoing continuity of care for their patients
outside of treatment and education centres.

CP/49'

Gráinne Smith is an author, writing from her considerable professional experience as a former teacher and primary head teacher working with children and families during tough times and easy, as well as her personal experience as a single family carer when her daughter was in a life-threatening condition with anorexia and her mother developed Alzheimer's.

Surviving Family Care Giving

Co-ordinating effective care through collaborative communication

Gráinne Smith

Routledge
Taylor & Francis Group

LONDON AND NEW YORK

First published 2015
by Routledge
27 Church Road, Hove, East Sussex, BN3 2FA

and by Routledge
711 Third Avenue, New York, NY 10017

*Routledge is an imprint of the Taylor & Francis Group,
an informa business*

© 2015 Gráinne Smith

British Library Cataloguing in Publication Data
A catalogue record for this book is available from the British Library

Library of Congress Cataloging in Publication Data
Smith, Gráinne, 1945-
Surviving family care giving : co-ordinating effective care through
collaborative communication / Gráinne Smith.
pages cm
1. Caregivers--Psychology. 2. Home nursing. 3. Interpersonal
communication. I. Title.
HV65.S65 2014
362'.0425--dc23
2014016426

ISBN: 978-0-415-63645-2 (hbk)
ISBN: 978-0-415-63646-9 (pbk)
ISBN: 978-1-315-75020-0 (ebk)

Typeset in New Century Schoolbook and Frutiger
by Saxon Graphics Ltd, Derby

Contents

Foreword

Many carers tell us that becoming a carer came as a complete surprise – and a shock. A car accident, a hospital diagnosis, the birth of a child – all of these things can turn an ordinary, normal life into an extraordinary and often difficult life.

Loneliness, isolation, depression and financial problems are all aspects of this new life that carers may have to deal with. Tough times indeed.

Surviving Family Care Giving sets out to address some of these issues. For many years, health and social care professionals have focused on treating patients or service users while the families of those people are left to get on with the daily job of caring. The conditions may vary, but families talk about the lack of relevant information and cite common problems of despair and exhaustion.

We estimate that throughout the UK one in 10 people currently find themselves in a caring role, but that figure will only increase as our population grows older. Current projections suggest that three in five people will find themselves in a caring role in the future.

Over the last few years there has been a greater acknowledgement of the vital role carers play in our society and the necessity of support for carers. This acknowledgement is welcome, but it is still the case that the problems faced by families while caring for someone can have profound effects.

We at Carers Trust recognise these profound effects. As the largest provider of comprehensive support services for carers, we reach close to half a million carers through a unique network of independently managed carers' services and interactive websites.

Gráinne Smith has used her personal and professional experience, bringing together the lessons she has learned to create useful suggestions and practical ideas which will help families to cope with caring.

Surviving Family Care Giving is mainly about communications – developing all-round support, finding information and the resources for your own situation, building more co-ordinated care and good, constructive conversations in the journey to family teamwork.

The book uses real-life examples from families coping with various conditions and ideas that can be adapted to fit the reader's own situation. It focuses on what carers can do to help themselves through telephone helplines, charities, self-help groups, relaxation therapies and more. It is, in short, a survival guide.

Andrew Cozens, Chair of Carers Trust

1

Beginnings and aims

In *Always on call, always concerned,* The Princess Royal Trust for Carers states:

> On average, 12% of the population provide unpaid care for a friend or family member; this increases to 18% for those aged 55–64, 16% for those aged 65–74, and 13% in those aged over 75.[1]

Just looking at those statistics, it's quite stunning to think how many people that could represent in every street, every village, town, city ... coping quietly, many without any outside support, information or resources. Stunning to wonder how many of our own neighbours could be 'carers' without our knowing.

In 1996 when my daughter Jay, 23, finally told me she had been diagnosed with 'anorexia nervosa, binge purge type', I had heard these words – but I had no idea what they meant, had never even heard the term 'carer'. So, feeling sick with worry, I made an appointment with our GP. I asked what I should be doing, or avoid doing, to help and support my daughter, who at the time looked like a walking skeleton – and the answer was *'You know as much as we do.'* This was not said unsympathetically; rather it was a statement of fact – in the 1990s, because most doctors at that time still believed in treating an adult as a single unit in isolation, very little if any information was offered to home carers who shared the lives of adult patients. Despite the very obvious change in her personality at home, whatever her emotional and mental health at the time, whatever her level of reasoning, Jay was legally an adult – and therefore *'in charge of her own life'.*

Years on, I know that some of the incidents I observed over those awful years could have been indications of heart problems – for instance, when Jay obviously had great difficulty climbing upstairs, and the several occasions when she fell downstairs – and I now know that low mineral levels due to eating problems can cause serious problems, e.g. lack of potassium can lead to heart failure. It is frightening to realise that former interpretations of 'confidentiality', which restricted communication to talking exclusively to the patient, in combination with my complete lack of knowledge of mental health problems or when to call for medical assistance, could have led to very serious consequences for my daughter.

We were extremely lucky. Once Jay reached her individual Major Turning Point and acknowledged her eating problems after five years, she then turned her considerable willpower and determination to fighting the illness rather than fighting those around her.

Yet mostly home carers simply cope, often over many years, often without mentioning their own particular difficulties. In some instances I'd known relatives, friends and colleagues for many years, but it was only when Jay became very obviously ill that they mentioned they'd also had experience of home caring for and supporting someone through very tough times – including three members of my large now-scattered-all-over-the-world family, who told me of experience with an eating disorder. This echoes stories from helplines, when I've talked to several people who were not only currently trying to support someone with an eating disorder, but who told me *'I've been through it before with my sister, or cousin, or neighbour … and I still don't know what to do to help'.*

Having failed to find that elusive practical book, I eventually chose some of my journal entries, searched for information far and wide, quoted many stories from other home carers I'd met or talked to by phone – and put together the book I'd been looking for, *'Anorexia and Bulimia in the Family'*.[2]

Thankfully despite my ignorance, and having to try to work out every day what might – just might – be helpful through those very tough times, Jay has survived. Over the years I have met several other parents whose children sadly did not survive, often due at least in part to a lack of co-ordinated care, with home carers lacking relevant information crucial to their at-home efforts.

'You know as much as we do...'

Learning from other carers

Over those years I gradually realised through talking to people from all sorts of connections that, although home carers were in a very wide range of situations and supporting people with a range of conditions or illnesses, there were common echoes which kept recurring – feelings of isolation, helplessness, despair at the lack of information and support, exhaustion from the relentless daily effort needed to continue.

Having recognised these themes in common despite the differences, I decided to write this book to try to offer support for the many home carers far and near, using my own experiences as a home carer and as a teacher, who has worked with so many families during tough times (as well as the good ones), and also as a member of the OU Development Group whose work feeds into the Social Work Honours degree. I will also quote from the experiences of carers I've talked to informally – in my own life and at work, at meetings, on helplines, at conferences – as well as providing quotes from interesting and relevant books and other sources I've found, sometimes in unexpected places.

This book is not an instruction book. Given the enormous range of conditions and illnesses, situations and circumstances in which carers find themselves, I reckon it would be impossible to write such a book. Rather than being about any particular condition or illness, this book is about building effective communication and how families and other home teams can offer important support through collaboration and co-ordinated efforts – which is important *whatever* the illness, condition or situation of the people involved.

What are the main aims of this book?

Having learned so much in my own home care-giving journey, I aim to share ideas and practical suggestions to support other home carers in their search for what they need in their own individual situations – which will probably be different from mine.

I also hope that professionals working in hospitals and health clinics, schools and treatment centres will read this book and think more about the lives of their own patients, clients and pupils outside their place of work.

Reading (and writing) this book

Given so many different health conditions, with so many individual variations involved even in the same diagnosis, different home situations, different family and individual approaches depending on so many factors, including ethnic, culture and religious backgrounds, as well as the influence of individual genetic inheritance – personal make-up and background, strengths and weaknesses, past experience and current situation – is this a simple 'one size fits all' book? *No.*

Words and interpretations

Many words which I've known for years, believing I understood their definitions, have caused me to pause. For instance, what is a 'family'? Apart from a group of beings such as cats or dogs, is it a social group consisting of parents and their offspring? Perhaps a group of persons related by blood? Or a group descended from a common ancestor? What of an 'extended family'? All the persons living in one household, perhaps related or unrelated, or some related and others unrelated, e.g. in cases of second or subsequent marriages where one or both partners already has children?

And what about 'communal living'? Students, or a group of friends or acquaintances, may also share a household perhaps simply for economic reasons – are they a 'family'? *Can* an unrelated group provide supportive home care?

Think of your own family, and the home situations of others. What would *your* definition be?

And in different places, different words may be used for those who provide support without professional services, whether they are a relative, a partner, a good friend, a volunteer – a carer, a home carer, a care giver, an informal carer, an employed carer…

Whether or not relationships are informal or through blood-lines, whether they are ancestral, informal or legally-binding, home situations are made up of individuals who happen to share accommodation and possibly certain bonds linked by current and/or past shared experiences, perhaps through marriage or blood relationships. Therefore I prefer to use 'home carer' to describe the committed individuals who support and care for another person in a home situation.

Challenging behaviour may be triggered in vulnerable people through frustration – perhaps through physical difficulties and loss of independence and activities, perhaps personal restrictions in understanding, or changes in personal interpretation and understanding situations. Perhaps they may have a lack of understanding of accepted social interactions, as is the case for those on the autistic spectrum, or a complete loss of understanding of time, memories of personal history and background, as in Alzheimer's. Serious problems can be caused by addictive/compulsive conditions such as alcoholism; symptoms, e.g. paranoia, can involve suspicion of other people and their motives and/or actions, intense denial and 'challenging behaviour' – all of which can add greatly to those tough times. Individual reactions and behaviour can be the problem, presenting a 'challenge' to other people ... although, as always, different people may have different feelings and reactions in any situation which they find 'challenging'.

What is *your* definition of 'challenging behaviour'? Is there a common definition which covers all possibilities? (See Chapter 4, *Challenging Behaviour.*)

Practical ideas and suggestions

This book offers ideas and suggestions for family and other home carers to discuss, and from there to develop their *own* team approach in their *own* situation – an approach which may be reviewed and adapted if and when necessary, *whatever* the home arrangements and bonds.

Chapters

Ordering the chapters was difficult. Which should come first, Information and Resources, or Communication? Confidentiality or Motivation? Or Carer Survival in tough times, to ensure that the best possible care continues? Where does teamwork fit into home life – and how? What of 'leadership'? Can everyone in a family or other home group offer the same level of support?

All these issues link and knit together in so many different individual family and home situations. There may be no easy answers, with different possible solutions in any situation – which of course may change with the circumstances and people involved, not to mention with possible changes or progress in the individual's health condition.

Different ways of reading this book

Straight through beginning to end, or dip in and out, or a mix of both? The choice is yours.

A personal learning curve...

While I would never wish to repeat those years of struggle when my daughter seemed to be changed out of all recognition, I recognise how much I've learned from the experiences of others caring at home. I also learned from professionals – medical, health and social work care workers – who have recognised that many informal carers can be a very valuable resource in supporting their patients or clients towards recovery. In some cases these outstanding individuals, working in various professions, have spoken out strongly about the past effects of ignoring these long-term home care givers – and at times they have faced criticism from others in their own professions who had yet to realise the possible home support that current theories and policies denied their patients.

Furthermore, I discovered that some doctors and other professionals, outside their often long working hours and commitments, are also 'family carers' in their home lives. Somehow I'd always had the impression that these families were immune from mental illness and other conditions involving challenging behaviour and tough times.

Throughout *Surviving Family Care Giving* I have quoted, in their own words, the experiences of many home carers and others I've talked to. Some preferred to use their own names, while others wished to remain anonymous.

'Tough Times'?

Difficult times where happiness and contentment, fun and laughter seem to have completely vanished, or perhaps may be seen only in occasional and isolated blinks, can involve and affect practically any aspect of life and living – physical and/ or mental health, communication, finance, crops, food and diet, accommodation, on the home front, at school, at work, in social activities. Often difficult times in one area of life will have a knock-on effect on other areas, as well as affecting the lives of close others sharing a household. For instance, finance will inevitably be affected when the main income changes after someone loses employment, or the main earner in the family develops a long-term illness or has a serious accident which limits mobility or capacity. Or perhaps a child or young person needs special care and one of the family gives up their employment to provide that support. Or due to changes in finance, mortgage payments can no longer be met and the whole family may have to move house.

Or... or... the possibilities are innumerable. Every story I've heard over all these years has been personal and individual, and yet there have often been many echoes of similar feelings. I know there are countless other versions. My own story is different from Wendy's, whose son has an acquired brain injury, whose story is very different from the experience of L, who is supporting his wife through multiple sclerosis. All these stories are different from that of S, who shares a flat with a friend who has bipolar disorder, and from J and B whose daughter has been undergoing treatment for bone cancer over several years... Each story is unique. Whatever your situation, wherever you are on your own personal care-and-support journey, I hope this book will offer you practical suggestions to help you work out and find what *you* need.

Notes

1 The Princess Royal Trust for Carers (2011), '*Always on call, always concerned*'.
2 Gráinne Smith (2004), *Anorexia and Bulimia in the Family*. John Wiley and Sons.

Home carers
Themes in common

Despite all the individual differences in home situations and approaches to the widely-differing health conditions of the loved ones being cared for, there are frequently echoes of common themes in carers' stories – the lack of relevant information and resources, feelings of inadequacy, feelings of exhaustion, helplessness, loneliness and isolation, and often despair.

Recently there has been more interest in home carers' experiences, and several newspapers have featured personal interviews with home carers – for instance, an interview[1] with Sarah Thomas and her parents described how Sarah had looked after her mother, who developed MS when Sarah was a small child; and then when she was a teenager her father developed a degenerative bone disease and fibromyalgia. Sarah says she's never known anything else. Now eighteen, she does household and any other chores, helps with medication, provides physical assistance when needed – and says that the worst aspect of her life has been bullying from her peers at school, and that even adults can sometimes be thoughtlessly unkind.

Estimates and statistics

Quoted alongside Sarah's story in that newspaper article were stark statistics: up to 700,000 children in the UK look after and help support parents or siblings with disabilities. The 'Kids Who Care' research from the BBC and a response from the Carers Trust[2] show that 27% of young carers under the age of fifteen miss school and experience educational difficulties, and 68% are bullied by their peers. Following Carers Trust research in partnership with the University of Nottingham into support (or otherwise) for young home carers, the organisation has developed a practical resource for use in schools, where teachers are often unaware of young people who try to juggle schoolwork with a home care-giving role.[3]

On their website, Carers UK state that:

- one in eight adults in the UK are carers
- 58% of carers are women and 42% are men
- there are an estimated six and a half million carers across the UK, with an anticipated increase to nine million by 2037
- over 1.3 million people provide over 50 hours of care a week
- one million carers provide care for more than one person.

In her book *Past Caring: The Beginning Not The End*[4] Audrey Jenkinson quotes a figure of over seven million carers in the UK today.

Whatever the exact numbers, many have coped without outside support for years and report that their own health has been badly affected by their ongoing 24-hours-a-day, 365-days-a-year commitment to a vulnerable family member, friend or partner. Unless others in the community have had personal experience of offering care during tough times, most people – even those living very nearby – have very little idea of what the reality of life as a home carer may involve.

Also, as many people don't recognise themselves as 'carers', these numbers may be inaccurate. However, *whatever* the statistics, family and other informal home carers' ongoing contributions to communities are at last beginning to be recognised, with Carers UK estimating that carers save the economy £119 billion per year.

In recent years, as social policy makers and unpaid home carers' services began to integrate, it was decided in the UK that services for this very valuable group of people should be specially identified for support services through their GP.

Before Jay became ill, among my friends and acquaintances there were several who had been quietly caring at home, but I had known very little about what was involved in caring for a relative with schizophrenia, bipolar disorder or severe arthritis, for example, let alone the wide variations involved in their experiences. I also discovered that some people I'd known as colleagues for years had had a home care role but had never mentioned it before – even in the late1990s, when my daughter's illness took over in our home, people rarely, if ever, spoke about mental health problems, especially when they affected their own families.

It was only through hearing the stories of other home carers at the NEEDS Scotland self-help group meetings at Aberdeen Cornhill Hospital that I began to realise how the same diagnosis could mean coping with situations and behaviour very different from Jay's, and therefore differing from my own experience as a home carer.

Similarities and differences

Whatever the similarities or differences in the health conditions, personal situations and experiences, another common theme is the feeling that somewhere along the path before a loved one's illness, there must have been something missed, something the home carers could have/should have done – or maybe not done? – to prevent or ease the difficulties and suffering involved in the long struggle to beat the disorder blighting a relation or friend's life.

Sadly, the enduring effects of the *It's All the Parents' Fault* theory, so strongly emphasised by medical 'experts' and well publicised over years, sometimes still persist despite much research into the role of genetic factors and individual reactions to personal stress.

I feel ill with worry and totally helpless, I just don't know what to do to help M and now I can't even visit her. I want to see her – keep thinking of her, how she must feel, wondering what's happening to her. She's been admitted to a specialist hospital hundreds of miles away from where we live.

And I'm angry too, so angry – angry with my husband. He insisted that she be treated as far away from here as possible. And he arranged it! He's a doctor, doesn't want any of his colleagues to find out about M's eating disorder. They all believe that it's all the parents' fault – mainly the mother's, of course.

Pamela

With over 30 years' experience in primary education and working with families valiantly trying to support one or more of their children through particular difficulties, much of this theory puzzled me because although there were exceptions, the vast majority of the parents I'd worked with were really concerned about their children and did their utmost to help them through their difficulties, whether with spelling and maths or disagreements and bullying. Every child is different, and reactions to personal stress are also very individual: where one child may react with tears and withdrawal from the situation causing them difficulty, even sometimes withdrawal from everyone around them, another may show their frustration by lashing out physically, including at teachers. Some may become very depressed. The same is true of teenagers and adults at any age and stage of life.

Personal stress, whether affecting children, teenagers, adults or senior citizens, is now acknowledged as a major trigger in many physical and mental health conditions. In a 1999 essay entitled *Stress and Illness,* D. Despues[5] of North California University states that there are three theories of stress: environmental, biological and psychological. Many interesting references are noted, including research into *Negative Life Events, Perceived Stress, Negative Affect and Susceptibility to the Common Cold.*[6] The NHS website www.nhs.uk/conditions/stress-anxiety-depression[7] also offers helpful suggestions to help deal with personal stress.

Stress certainly seemed to trigger major change in Jay. All through breast feeding, childhood and as a teenager I'd known her by her well-deserved nickname Tigger (because she was so bouncy, outgoing and great fun), but she changed dramatically when she struggled to cope and began having eating problems, leading eventually to her diagnosis. 'Tigger' vanished completely.

Having discovered the theories about 'bad parenting' and abuse, in common with so many other parents I've talked to I spent many hours trying to work out what I could have – should have? – done differently to save my child such suffering.

How did we get here? – theories and research

Years later in 2005, when I was accidentally sent two research questionnaires from Birmingham University School of Psychology, I began to get an idea of how such theories might have been somehow 'proved' by research. The questionnaire was not intended for families supporting someone with an eating disorder, but for people struggling with eating disorders themselves. The debrief which accompanied the questionnaires stated: *'This research proposes that childhood abuse indirectly affects eating attitudes through another variable, core beliefs.'* Both questionnaires asked for limited choice answers – all negative, without exception – about personality and home environment.

For instance, from the 75 statements given for Personality:

Most of the time I haven't had someone to nurture me, or care deeply about everything that happens to me.

I don't belong; I'm a loner.

I always feel on the outside of groups.

I'm unworthy of the love, attention, and respect of others.

I feel that I'm not lovable.

I'm incompetent when it comes to achievement.

If you ask someone who is already stressed by unhappy experiences such endlessly negative questions, without any discussion and with no opportunity to note any positive experiences, what are the results most likely to be?

A few more from the 91 questions related to Home Environment:

Did your parents yell at you?

Did you have traumatic sexual experiences when you were a child or teenager?

How often were you left alone at home as a child?

Did your relationship with your parents ever involve a sexual experience?

Were you physically mistreated as a child or teenager?

Was your childhood stressful?

As a child were you ever punished in unusual ways, e.g. locked in a closet for a long time or being tied up?

Were there traumatic or upsetting sexual experiences when you were a child or teenager that you couldn't speak to adults about?

When either of your parents was intoxicated, were you ever afraid of being sexually mistreated?

Did your parents blame you for things you didn't do?

Did you ever witness the sexual mistreatment of another family member?

Not a single reference to even the smallest possibility of happiness, unreserved warmth, gifts, happiness – let alone love – shown by *any* member of the family.

Few people grow up in absolutely ideal circumstances and remain 100% happy all the time ... is this possible? There may have been some unhappy or difficult experiences for *any* individual, within *any* family. There may indeed be an exceptionally difficult personality or two to cope with. However, this research is focused solely on misery and bad experiences, stressing ill-treatment, unhappiness, difficult experiences – unrelenting negativity, with no interest at all in anyone who might have supported, let alone loved, the person.

An explanation? A bit of background to Western health treatment approaches

Freud, Klein and Jung are all familiar and frequently-quoted names in psychology, whose theories gave core insights into human nature and noted how individuals can be greatly affected by early experiences, including those that occur within their family.

Unfortunately, rather than leading to further research and exploration, these initial theories were then stretched by many in a negative way to become general theories. As Jad Adams quotes in his *Guardian* review of *Medical Muses: Hysteria in Nineteenth-Century Paris'* by Asti Hustvedt:[8] '*All three clinical models impose a theoretically based framework which de-emphasises context and gives primacy to professional interpretation.*' Hustvedt goes on to show how, while Freud, Klein and Jung may be the most familiar names in psychology, many others also built similar theories which became widely accepted, mostly without question, and were applied generally to all patients who met the current medical criteria of diagnosis for a particular condition.

It seems that much research over many years has been based on that one theory, of relentlessly negative family behaviour towards the individual who is driven into illness. Speaking only to an individual patient or client, without any contact with family members, the theory so often promoted over many years became widely accepted.

'Standing in someone else's shoes'

Listening to real experiences told by people who have lived through them – indeed, who are often still living through them – can be gruelling as well as moving. Fortunately, in addition to reading and debating academic theories, over recent years some professionals have *listened to* questions, *listened to* individual stories ... and have begun to question the blame-and-shame theories.

Different situations, similar feelings

Trying to be a Carer at home is like trying to do a jigsaw blindfolded. There are always some of the pieces missing. I just wish someone would sit down with me and tell me the best thing to do when ...

There are so many times every day when I'd like to ask someone – anyone – what's best to do.

John

In her article *My dad, my little boy* Anna May Mangan[9] describes a similar story of her own family feelings when, after weeks of daily vigils at his bedside, her father opened his eyes – and recognised no-one; his home meant nothing to him. With the mental age of a toddler, he needed constant 24/7 supervision – and he also had a young child's lack of understanding of the consequences of actions. For instance, one day she found him building a pyramid of sticks and paper on the foot of his bed, ready to set fire to it with his cigarette lighter, because his 'feet were lollipops in bed'. She also describes the day when the police called to ask her to collect him after he'd been found

Feelings of isolation

fast asleep on a neighbour's bed after he'd gone out for a walk, felt tired, and seen an open door as an invitation while she had been chatting to the neighbour. He was described as 'certainly the naughtiest toddler in town'.

She hasn't eaten anything all week. You know it's going to be a tough evening. She feels faint, sick, looks like a ghost – the worst bit is, you can't do a thing to help. Whatever you say or do, she looks at you with contempt – all her gentleness, her smiles and jokes, all gone. She can be so aggressive sometimes. Her friends don't come round any more.

She has to have a shower same time every night. The water runs and runs – sometimes the hot water runs out and all hell breaks loose. Shouting, screaming, hitting. Like a nightmare. Every night. Every single day. We're all shattered, what has happened to our daughter? How long can this go on?

She's obsessed with cleanliness and cleaning – until her energy runs out. Then everybody is on tenterhooks, knowing it'll all start over again, wondering when.

Frances

Grieving for and missing the person you knew is another recurring theme

The phone rang and the voice said 'Your husband has been in a RTA' – I now know, jargon for Road Transport Accident. He didn't recognise me anymore, or any of his family either. In a split second the person he had been was wiped out, just his body left. And our whole lives changed completely. He doesn't remember anything about our lives together. The doctors assessed his mental age as that of a toddler, that's younger than his grandchildren. The worst bit every day is waking up; he asks who I am. I miss him so much – the man I knew for so many years. Every morning. It just breaks my heart, for him. For me too, sometimes.

Patricia

I've done the grieving for my wife, I'll never get her back. We've lost the future we looked forward to, we thought we'd have. It's like living in a nightmare.

Peter

There's no way of taking the dementia away, making my mum remember who she is and who I am ... that's a huge fight on its own, the person she really was is gone. But why do I have to struggle to get the correct advice or medication, to find the right help to allow my mum to get through this with as much dignity as possible? Why?

Michael

I felt so helpless ... what are you supposed to do when your son, aged 20, starts crawling up and down stairs? He was diagnosed with schizophrenic-affective disorder in his second year of university. We're now 16 years on and he still denies his illness.

What are you supposed to do when he arrives from London at the bus station wearing a jumper – with his legs in the sleeves, and waving a razor blade? And he's lost his passport, lost his money, lost his luggage but picked up some other luggage. What are you supposed to do when he's so unpredictable and seems very aggressive, provokes people he says 'look' at him? At home, we once used dining chairs to defend ourselves. He doesn't seem to realise people feel he's being aggressive, to the extent of getting himself arrested.

What comes next? What about the rest of our family? We're all exhausted, struggling ... we want to help our son, he's just not the person he was...

It's way outside our experience, what are we supposed to do?

James

The hardest thing is that she's just not the same person, the Maggie I knew has gone. It's like a bereavement but you can't grieve – it's not like when my dad died.

Sandra

Talking to someone with experience of different kinds of grief and feelings of bereavement, or talking to others who have come through similar feelings, may help when you're going through these really tough emotional times.

Financial situations

Being in an easier financial situation is certainly a great help with practical matters such as finding and funding extra help at home, trained babysitters and support ... but none at all when Joe Public feels that somehow your status as a carer also confers a very thick skin impervious to 'jokes' about your child told by cheap comedians, and accusations from cruel and thoughtless magazines and newspapers that you somehow caused their problems. For instance, Katie Price, glamour model and media celebrity, told the story of how she and her son Harvey – who *'has septo-optic dysplasia which causes blindness and growth hormone deficiency; Prader-Willi syndrome, a genetic disorder that means that he is likely to eat to excess and is prone to obesity and diabetes; as well as ADHD and autism'*[10] – were the butt of 'jokes' when a well-known comedian thought it was funny to talk about them to his audience. In other words, mindless and unacceptable bullying behaviour.

Of that comedian, Katie Price said that if his wife or kids were in an accident and got paralysed from the neck down, it would absolutely change his life, *'and I'm sure he'd think twice about making jokes about people who can't answer back'*. Sadly, because Joe Public reads tabloids and watches such comedians on TV, and because he can't imagine the same thing happening to his own loved ones, some people think it's ok to inflict similar pain on others.

Dealing with bullies – a suitable response?

Many home carers have spoken of unpleasant comments from neighbours or people they meet in the street or shops. After undertaking research into bullying at school, Carers Trust has developed support resources, e.g. *Supporting Young Carers: A Resource for Schools*.[11]

If you (or anyone you know) has experience of such ignorance and unpleasant behaviour, having a response ready will hopefully make the speaker pause to think about how they would feel if any of their family members were in similar circumstances. *How would you feel if your son (or daughter, mum, dad, sister...) had similar problems? If you couldn't do the things you can do now?* Try to be prepared – think of your own response and what you would like to say, practice before you may need it – and then walk away. Said calmly, and repeated if necessary, this kind of response can be much more powerful than anger, no matter how justified, and it may stop the unkind person in their tracks.

And if the unpleasant bullying behaviour continues? Consider reporting it to a relevant authority: the police, a community group, or a teacher in the case of juveniles.

Feelings of inadequacy

To return to Anna May Mangan's series of articles in the *Guardian*, *My dad, my little boy*, she also describes how, following his peaceful death from cancer eight years after his accident, she relived all the meals she'd cooked for him, all the drugs she'd administered, every wash she'd given him – and how her main feeling was guilt. She echoes the words of so many other care givers: *'Could I have done better? Being a carer is the loneliest job in the world.'*

> *I keep wondering if there was something I should have noticed, maybe information I should have known, could have done differently, which might have saved my husband such suffering. I've spent hours and hours going over all sorts of things, our life together.*
>
> Fiona

> *We really needed the money to survive – but maybe if I hadn't gone out to work, maybe John would still be with us. I thought he was fine, I should have realised. If only I'd realised how depressed he was.*
>
> Derek

Whatever the situation, no matter how much support a home carer has offered, 24/7 and 365 days a year, often giving up their own lives, careers, financial security and social life along the way, they frequently feel that they somehow could and should have done more.

A clear diagnosis – or not?

This is another recurring theme which can cause much frustration. With each human being made up of a complex and individual mix of genes plus experience and background, perhaps it is inevitable that the same can be said of any individual when it comes to diagnosis. For those human beings whose mix of symptoms fits no single diagnosis – or 'label' – the consequences can be far-reaching. Also, developing one condition does not imply immunity to other conditions that may develop alongside and which can create further complications for the individual at the centre, their professional staff and, of course, their home carers.

There are thousands of years of medical exploration and debate, research and hefty tomes of written details, plus developments in modern medicines, techniques, various technologies as well as many therapies – surely diagnosis in the early twenty-first century should be fairly straight-forward, yes?

Not quite so simple. Whatever the particular illness or condition, there are indeed individuals who present classic symptoms and for whom diagnosis is straightforward, meaning that appropriate treatment can then be offered. There are others who present many of those same features plus a few individual variations, or perhaps they present most of the main features but not others. For these people, a diagnosis may still be made and appropriate treatment offered. However, there are others who present a mix of features and symptoms which seem to fit several possible diagnoses ... and who fit no single departmental specialism.

Much time may be lost as an individual waits for an appointment, only to find that after undergoing tests and answering questions and many notes being taken, heads are shaken and the patient is referred to another department for further investigation. More weeks or months may pass before an appointment can be made for different tests. Unfortunately this pattern may be repeated, sometimes several times before a diagnosis is arrived at. A straightforward and clear-cut diagnosis is a gift, which makes life so much simpler for doctor and treatment teams – and also in many ways for the individual patients they treat, and their families.

Physical or emotional problems? Or a mix?

Diagnosis seems much simpler when physical symptoms are visible, or when they can be found and identified with close examination using X-ray or scans. It is much more difficult when the person appears physically in good health but displays emotional problems, distorted thinking or uncontrollable behaviour which may be present only in certain personally-stressful situations.

> *By 13 C had been seen by lots of people, there was no continuity. Every time we saw someone different, we'd go through the same story again and again and again, never got anywhere. Then eventually a speech therapist suggested he be seen by an occupational therapist ... who suggested dyspraxia ... and obsessive compulsive disorder ... and ADHD ... and Tourette's. A friend who has family experience of Asperger's syndrome thought some of C's behaviour could be similar...*

From a personal interview with Sheila,
quoted in full in *Families, Carers and Professionals:
Building Constructive Conversations.*[12]

Sheila's story is just one of many I've come across over many years in education and through friends, colleagues, acquaintances. An explanation for the thinking behind this was given to me by a medical friend: *'No particular diagnosis can be made because the individual does not fit the list of symptoms listed for any one particular condition.'* In Western medicine in particular, after training many, if not most, doctors and nurses specialise in a specific area of medicine and often in a particular condition.

Individual situations – and responses

Another frequent question: *'Why does no-one believe me when I describe behaviour at home?'*

> *Please would you write a letter about N's behaviour in school? The consultant doesn't believe me when I talk about her behaviour at home – N is quiet in his office. What can I do? Nobody believes me!*

Mrs B

I had known N well for almost three years at that time, and her out-of-control and difficult behaviour had caused many problems at break time, with similar behaviour in games lessons and sometimes in class – although in class when absorbed in an activity N liked and understood, she could also be a model pupil. I was happy to write a letter of support for Mrs B to give to the consultant.

Depending on situation and surroundings, individual expectations, who is present at the time, from well-known people to unfamiliar contacts, people often behave differently in particular situations. A child may behave very differently at home; with individual family members present or not; in class; in the playground; in physical education; with friends and peer groups; with other social groups; with strangers or people they don't know well; with an individual adult or in a group; with individual teachers; with new and unfamiliar staff... Not to mention according to varying energy levels, adequate sleep or not, diet and state of health, and various other personal factors.

To complicate matters even further, an individual may also change dramatically in response to circumstances. These may involve a personally stressful event which triggers certain behaviours or even illness, or it may be something which reminds the person of such an event – this may not always be obvious to other people, who respond differently and may regard something that can greatly stress another person as trivial.

A personal example here – at school once I talked about how stressful I found being shouted at by K's irate mum, who had been asked by the cook to pay for a dinner ticket to replace one K had lost, one of a series of tickets lost by K. In response a colleague said that he really enjoyed 'a good run-in', and he'd 'never been bested yet'. Something that had caused me a sleepless night or more only served to get the adrenaline flowing for my colleague!

Denial of problems?

In eating disorders a mix of physical and mental health factors sometimes makes diagnosis very difficult. Added to an already complex picture of these devastating illnesses with compulsive/

obsessive/addictive features which can quickly become chronic, common factors include a complete denial of any problem and a refusal of any suggested treatment due to distorted thinking. *I'm not ill, so why do you think I need treatment? I'm not ill, how dare you suggest I am – I won't comply with your treatment!* Denial is frequently a feature of alcoholism, drug addiction and other addictive/compulsive conditions.

All of which adds greatly to the difficulties for individuals urgently needing treatment – and, of course, to the difficulties of home carers who have ringside seats.

Whatever the condition, in the best circumstances a diagnosis seems to open so many doors

For children and adolescents treatment may be possible, may be offered. New avenues may be suggested for exploration. Reading material may be suggested, charity contacts and useful websites may be noted, and possibly extra support may be offered to help in home situations. In school, special account may be taken of particular difficulties and more support may be possible – perhaps in the classroom, or more supervision in the playground, or extra tuition in certain curricular areas.

Legally an adult?

Even now, when a diagnosis has been made family and other home carers of legally-adult patients often face major continuing difficulties – as well as the frustration of knowing there are probably several keys to appropriate helpful information, but these are not shared with informal care givers.

P's mother was having increasing difficulty in coping and living independently. As P was the only family member with no dependents to support, he gave up his own home and many activities and moved in to help his mother. He found her behaviour extremely difficult to cope with at times, and got little sleep due to his mother's erratic sleep patterns. He thought – perhaps Alzheimer's?

P felt more and more isolated as his mother's behaviour caused more and more problems at home and for neighbours.

When he asked their GP for any information on his mother's condition and suggestions about how best to respond to her behaviour, and how to cope, he was told that confidentiality meant that no information could be given. P's mother's condition continued to deteriorate, and P continued to cope – just. He was offered 'a day off each week' when his mother was taken into local respite care. Three days off were allowed for him to travel to attend his brother's funeral.

One day a home care-giver accidentally left a folder of notes behind. P opened the folder – and read that his mother had been diagnosed with schizophrenia.

N

Home carers of adults are frequently expected to 'work in the dark'. Without a diagnosis, without relevant information about the condition plus the right resources including personal support, home carers are seriously handicapped.

Notes

1 *Guardian* Family section, 2.02.13, interview with Sarah Thomas and her parents.
2 www.carers.org/press-release/national-young-carers-coalitions-response-bbc-'kids-who-care'-research (Accessed on 15/5/2014).
3 www.carers.org (Accessed on 15/5/2014).
4 Jenkinson, A. (2003) *Past Caring: The Beginning Not The End.* Promenade Publishing.
5 Despues, D. (1999) *Stress and Illness.* Essay, North California University. Available at www.csun.edu (Accessed on 15/5/2014).
6 Cohen, S., Tyrrell, D., and Smith, A. P. (1993) *Negative Life Events, Perceived Stress, Negative Affect and Susceptibility to the Common Cold.* Journal of Personality and Social Psychology, Vol 64.
7 www.nhs.uk/conditions/stress-anxiety-depression (Accessed on 15/5/2014).
8 Hustvedt, A. (2012) *Medical Muses: Hysteria in Nineteenth-Century Paris.* Bloomsbury.
9 Mangan, A. M. (2012) *My dad, my little boy. Guardian* Family, 25.08.12.
10 Price, K. (2012) Interview, *Guardian* Weekend, 29.9.12.
11 Carers Trust *'Supporting Young Carers: A resource for schools'.*
12 Smith, G. (2007) *Families, Carers and Professionals: Building Constructive Conversations.* John Wiley and Sons, UK.

3

Collaborative care

Collaborative care in brief:

Why? To provide better all-round care and support, 24 hours a day, 365 days a year, for the vulnerable people at the centre of all our efforts.

When? As and when needed, from the first changes noticed in an individual's behaviour and home carers' recognition of symptoms, through to recognising signs of possible relapse. You possibly already have some other thoughts relating to your own particular situation?

Who? Everyone involved in day-to-day care – professionals, family and other 'home team' members including friends or neighbours.

Where? Wherever needed:

- within the home situation and 'the wider world' of the individual
- in work or education
- social and all other activities in the 'wider world' of the individual.

And how? With much goodwill, through exploring and developing the most effective ways of communication and co-ordination within family and professional teams as above, and through collaboration between professional/family/informal home carers.

Over recent years in Western medicine it has been recognised and acknowledged that support for vulnerable individuals can be much more effective if it is carried out through collaborative care with everyone involved on a day-today basis. In other words, with everyone 'singing from the same song sheet' – or through teamwork, however tough the times. This means building a constructive family (or 'home team') as well as professional/home communication, cooperation and collaboration. This applies to all conditions, *whatever* the home situation, *whatever* an individual needs.

Main benefits of collaborative care?

- More effective all-round care and support, with continuity 24 hours a day, 365 days a year.
- The alternative? A scattergun approach, with short periods of intensive 'professional' therapy in surroundings detached from the individual's everyday life and the rest of that individual's time spent in the Real World. No matter how much goodwill family members and other informal carers have, without relevant information very few are adequately equipped to offer informed support, often on a long-term basis.
- Daily observations by close contacts can be invaluable for helping to alert professionals to the need for an increased level of care and support. By acknowledging and listening to these observations, and acting earlier rather than later, a setback or relapse may be restricted to a slight dip rather than a major dive. In some cases home carers might notice mood and behaviour changes which may be the beginning of (for example) a psychotic episode, severe depression and suicidal thoughts, losing control and violent or dangerous behaviour. Effective professional reactions to such information, and increased support if and when needed, may prevent tragedy and even save lives.

Effects of past beliefs and practice

With an emphasis over many years on the theory that all emotional and mental health problems (some physical conditions too) were the fault of the family and particularly the mother, in the past it was very easy to believe all sorts of theories and not look any further. This led not only to difficult repercussions within families and a lack of relevant information about what to do – or what to avoid doing – but also to a lack of support in very difficult circumstances affecting the whole household, and an absence of relevant information for the professionals treating the individual. Of course, there was also little or no continuity and co-ordination of care for the vulnerable people at the centre.

Thankfully, in more recent years some outstanding professionals have realised and acknowledged the effects of outdated practices. For instance, writing about *Problems in society, problems in psychiatry,* Hutchinson and Hickling state: 'The interaction of social and biological processes may explain behaviour at an individual level, but greater credence must also be given to an understanding of social dynamics, in particular how power relationships within a society can give rise to psychosocial pathology. Until psychiatry recognises its responsibility in this way, and abandons some of its outdated assumptions, it will continue to be seen as a perpetrator of social abuse rather than an instrument of care and rehabilitation for those who already feel excluded by the society in which they live.'[1]

Past treatments

Going back only a relatively short time in history, many treatments that were developed for people who didn't conform to the accepted rules in whatever society they belonged can now be recognised as very detrimental to the patient. For instance, being locked in a cellar without food or water could cause actual physical harm as well as being extremely distressing. The influence of these theories was far-reaching, often extended way beyond the treatment of 'challenging conditions'. For more about how patients with mental health problems were treated in the past, read *Mad in America* by Robert Whitaker.[2]

Likewise, the theories that professionals were somehow protecting their patients by withholding information about diagnosis, and that any contact with family members or friends would be interpreted by patients as breach of confidentiality, were widely accepted for many years. With no contact with a patient's family, hearing only one interpretation – possibly distorted by the effects of illness – of his or her life outside the clinic or hospital, professionals lacked much relevant information about their patients. In addition, by ignoring a patient's life outside treatment, these individuals were also denied even the thought and possibility that some people in their life outside cared very much about them and wanted to offer help and support.

In journalism too the focus and stress have been almost exclusively on bad news...

> Journalists need experts as badly as experts need journalists. Every day there are newspaper pages and television newscasts to be filled, and an expert who can deliver a jarring piece of wisdom is always welcome. Working together, journalists and experts are the architects of much conventional wisdom.[3]

So convinced were many therapists of the 'Shame and Blame the Parents' theory, they often dedicated whole hours of therapy to encouraging patients to question all the incidents of their childhood and the actions of their parents, to find the reason for that person's recent emotional and mental health:

> *I couldn't remember any incident with my parents which he could call abuse or abusive ... he just didn't seem to believe me, kept on asking me. Then he said I must have blocked out what happened.*
>
> B, personal contact

Whole books have also been devoted to that same conviction. Research was sometimes based on assumptions, with questions distorted to prove a particular point (see Chapter 2, Birmingham University Psychology questionnaire). Furthermore, when research didn't prove what the researcher had set out to prove, it was sometimes quietly shelved and remained unpublished.

The consequences? Often an unquestioning belief in the announcements of 'experts' – in many other fields as well as medicine – led to very wrong assumptions with no consideration given to other possibilities. Knowing about these assumptions, families often avoided talking about relatives who were being treated for mental health and many other disabling conditions.

> *Out walking with a friend, I mentioned that my brother was in hospital and had been diagnosed with schizophrenia and*

my friend looked very surprised. Then he nodded and told me that his cousin had schizophrenia and had been hospitalised several times ... I'd known my friend and some of his family for years and his cousin's illness had never been mentioned.

Julie

Down's syndrome, autism, physical and mental handicaps, depression and many other conditions ... because of the stress on the Shame and Blame theory, many – most? – family members have been reluctant to talk about the problems to acquaintances or colleagues. Further, many families have experience of more than one member born with, or later developing, difficult and often challenging long-term conditions. Sometimes this will occur in a single family or in a generation, and sometimes when a particular condition develops, with a bit of research into earlier generations it is found that the same condition also occurred.

Accusations based on assumptions

Unfortunately there are indeed people who deliberately abuse their own children, and there are others who hit out blindly in the heat of the moment. However, with the Shame and Blame theory so widely accepted, sadly there have also been instances of accusations based solely on assumptions. To quote just one situation – Sir Roy Meadow, a paediatrician, developed the theory of Munchausen's syndrome by proxy, a condition which allegedly leads parents to harm their children in order to draw attention to themselves. The theory was finally discredited after the release from prison of three mothers who had all lost babies to cot death, and who were then found guilty of murder on the basis of Meadow's suggestions that the odds of losing more than one child to cot death were completely unrealistic. Later, newspapers reported the whole story and quoted the case of Trupti Patel from 2003,[4] who was accused of suffocating three of her babies and who was cleared of deliberately murdering her children when it emerged during her trial that Mrs Patel's maternal grandmother had tragically lost five children in early infancy, suggesting that a genetic disorder could account for their deaths.

Brittle bone disease (osteogenesis imperfecta) is another problem which has sometimes led to families being wrongly accused. To quote just one article, Sally Shannon states that *'Broken bones are often the first signs of disease.'*[5] Also, Heller an Shapiro, the executive director of the Osteogenesis Imperfecta Foundation, states: *'I've had parents tell me about breaking a baby's leg when lifting them by the ankles to change a diaper. We get calls about false accusations of abuse all the time.'*[6]

Recent change and progress

In education, for many years parents felt there was a line drawn at the main school door over which they hesitated to step, but at the same time it was also recognised as helpful when a pupil had someone at home checking that homework was completed and so on. Later, many schools adopted 'homework books', where a child noted down what was required for practice at home – e.g. reading homework, maths, environmental studies – and which parents were expected to supervise and then sign. Today, parents are often asked to help with outings, relevant projects and research connected with the curriculum; and pupils may be elected as part of a Class Council involving representatives from each class who are willing to reflect classmates' views. All of this is aimed at providing a practical preparation for life in today's world.

Also, medical research has begun to change focus, often led by outstanding professionals who are willing to stand up and publicly disagree with colleagues who cling to the outdated theories (e.g. Freudian) on which they have often based many years of their career. Alternative possibilities are now being actively acknowledged and explored, with training in several professions beginning to include *how* families may be a source of support ... *if* they know what to do, what to try to avoid doing, and when, who and how to ask for help.

'New' training ideas

In this new dawn, in addition to presenting lectures and a recommended reading list and possibly taking part in research interspersed with 'on the ground' practical experience under supervision, some course designers have also recruited people with direct experience to help plan a more collaborative approach in professional areas such as:

- education
- medicine, nursing, social work, community work
- between different professional teams involved in care plans.

For instance, the Open University Social Work Department, along with other social care departments, has recruited people to be part of a 'Service Users and Carers Development Group', a fascinating mix of family care givers and 'service users' who, in the current Scottish group, have between them personal experience of a wide range of long-term conditions including multiple sclerosis, schizophrenia, spina bifida, eating disorders, Turner's Syndrome and Acquired Brain Injury. The work of these groups feeds directly into the OU Honours Social Work and Nursing degree training courses.[7] Work has recently started on building an archive of recorded interviews and podcasts with people reporting their personal experiences of the conditions they live with, and describing what helped and what could have been more helpful. Put together, this is the beginning of an important training resource.

In this group I also meet other family carers who express similar feelings to my own when I was a home carer, and I hear echoes of the several themes so common in a very wide range of health conditions. Being involved in the *Telling our Story* project, which summarises the aims and work of the OU group over its initial five years, was fascinating and further confirmed the existence of those echoes and themes I'd become conscious of and which I outlined in Chapter 2.

Also, at the Maudsley Hospital in London recent developments in training have included creating practical CDs involving family carers and service users, who are also involved in training workshops.[8]

Major changes underway

Medical practitioners such as Kim T. Mueser PhD and Susan Gingerich MSW acknowledge that *'Most models (of treatment), in fact, viewed the family as a source of "toxins" rather than help'.*[9] John Read, Loren R. Mosher and Richard Benstall tell more about the development of treatments (e.g. electro-convulsive therapy or ECT), discussing the beliefs and assumptions behind them and how medical approaches and treatments have greatly changed in recent years – including a chapter on *'Family therapy and schizophrenia: replacing ideology with openness'.*[10]

Although these authors were writing about schizophrenia, this description of common approaches and experiences in mental health treatment, and the deliberate exclusion over many years of families from any contact with services treating their loved ones, could be equally applied to other illnesses and conditions.

Journalists have also highlighted recent changes in beliefs and approaches:

> The eating disorder anorexia nervosa could be caused by a brain dysfunction, rather than social pressures, a study shows. Researchers at St George's Hospital in Tooting, south London, found sufferers have an abnormality in the blood flow to an area of the brain which affects body image. In results presented at an international conference in London, the researchers say this points to a biological cause for the condition.[11]

Similar research has now been carried out for many health conditions, leading to very changed attitudes in medical approaches:

> Families and friends are the main Carers of most patients living outside hospital. It is their role to encourage suitable behaviours, provide psychological support, and encourage adherence to treatment. They have to tolerate unusual and challenging behaviour or social withdrawal. Prolonged involvement in care is stressful, and the impact of mental illness on both Carers and the extended family should not be underestimated. The welfare of Carers should be considered within a patient's care plan, and appropriate counselling or respite organised if necessary.[12]

Also, from *Personal Recovery and Mental Illness*[13] by Dr Mike Slade:

> The lack of hope has toxic consequences. The self-fulfilling nature of being told by an expert that you'll never be able to work, or live independently, or have children or be treatment-free is profoundly damaging. The reason that clinicians should never make these statements is not some vague notion of withholding damaging information. It is because these statements are often wrong.

Dr Slade's '100 ways to support recovery',[14] which is free to download, also offers explanations of the background to past practices and hope for the future, along with constructive suggestions including 10 recovery principles from the Yale Program for Recovery and Community Health:[15]

Care is Recovery-oriented
Strength-based
Community-focused
Person-centred
Allows for reciprocity in relationships
Culturally responsive
Grounded in the person's life context
Relationally mediated
Optimises natural supports.

Rather than passive compliance, recovery treatments foster taking responsibility and are based on an individual's hopes and dreams, with the provider adapting to the individual and fostering empowerment and self-management.

Finally, from Professor Glenn Waller's 2010 endorsement of *The Clinician's Guide to Collaborative Caring in Eating Disorders: The new Maudsley method*:

> ... this book's biggest contribution is the way in which it stresses that clinicians should see the family as a resource (rather than a nuisance or an irrelevance).[16]

Major changes indeed! What is more, this 'new' framework applies to anyone and everyone.

Above all, valuing the person as a human being

Glenn Waller's endorsement cited above stresses that families can be seen as a resource, Mike Slade also emphasises *'giving hope, a personal journey stressing unique identity, connections to others, and life within own social environment'*,[17] and in their book for clinicians, Janet Treasure, Ulrike Schmidt and Pam McDonald state that *'Eating disorders can – and do – put tremendous demands on the coping abilities of family members. Carers and other family members are usually the main support for the sufferer'*.[18]

Though situations, circumstances and tough times may differ widely, the same words are true in relation to other conditions and illnesses.

Can everyone really provide the same level of support? All family and other informal home carers?

Most family members very much want to support other family members. *Most* family members, young and old, will do their very best to offer good support, especially when given relevant information about what to do and what to try to avoid, and also knowing when to call for help. However, for various reasons, in common with people working in the caring professions, some people are able to provide more effective personal support than others. The ability to study and remember theories – and, in professional life, pass exams and gain qualifications – is very different from being able to relate to others, empathising with their difficulties and working out practical ways to help.

There are also a few who will stay around during very tough times in a home situation only through some sense of 'duty', feeling personally resentful about what they see as a very unfair hand dealt to them by Fate. Others, while they support financially, may feel unable to cope with physical or emotional realities they find difficult, and withdraw into themselves. Also, sadly, there are some who simply can't cope with the long-term effects on their own lives and leave the vulnerable person to fend for themselves.

A few family and other home groups struggle to provide the individual support needed. This can be for various reasons, e.g. a lack of understanding, a lack of resources, or a lack of empathy.

Good communication is a very important key to the quality of care and support – within the family and home environment, within and between professional teams (often more than one team may be involved in different aspects of an individual's care) and between professional and home carers.

All sorts of factors may present trip wires – for instance, there may be communication difficulties due to different backgrounds and understanding, between people from different cultures, and even between people from other areas of one's own country. (See Chapter 6, *Communication*.)

Effects of stress and fatigue on concentration

Whether someone is a professional or a home carer, care can also sometimes fluctuate depending on levels of tiredness and concentration. Sometimes past experiences intrude on present reactions; sometimes current events in other areas of an individual's life intrude, e.g. work difficulties, or money, or any number of other personal problems. These can all have a negative impact on patience and the ability to find the right words.

Recognisable personality approaches?

Perhaps you recognise *Kangaroo*, who always wants to protect and shield from possible problems and consequences of the loved one's behaviour or choices, who often ignores unacceptable behaviour even when it significantly affects other people, and who makes excuses for the individual? Perhaps you've met *Rhino*, who charges in with all the answers and has never considered listening to the thoughts and feelings of others? Or *Jellyfish*, who lives in a heightened emotional state, dissolves easily into tears, is agitated with doubt, and caves in at the least sign of difficulty? However, *Ostrich* simply sticks his head in the sand and refuses to even acknowledge a changed and unwanted situation. All these are approaches which are possibly exaggerated by a lack of knowledge of the condition involved, let alone about long-term caring in tough times.

Finally, *Dolphin* may swim alongside giving encouragement, or might lead the way for a time, falling back and staying out of sight when appropriate to allow another to find their own way, while still being aware of possible pitfalls and ready to respond as needed. Perhaps you can think of some more personality descriptions from the world of animals, sea creatures, birds?

Although Kangaroo, Dolphin, Rhino, Jellyfish and Ostrich were used as a light-hearted way of outlining recognisable personality descriptions in *Skills-based Caring for a Loved One with an Eating Disorder*,[19] these individual character approaches, and possibly others, are often recognised by home carers coping with other very different conditions.

However, whatever the condition, whatever the tough times, whatever happens, collaborative care through all-round teamwork can achieve wonders that otherwise may not be possible. And no matter how much goodwill they feel, very few people are naturally equipped to be a Dolphin, always giving constant calm encouragement, swimming alongside, leading the way or falling back as needed – all while still being aware of possible pitfalls and ready to respond if necessary.

What if... a young person, legally an adult, wants to live independently – but needs extra support to ensure that they're safe and can cope? Just one story of collaborative care in very tough times was given to me by Wendy, Gavin's mum.

> *Gavin is an intelligent man who sustained and survived a severe brain injury. After hospital treatment Gavin returned home, and later decided that as he was legally an adult he wanted to have his own place and live independently.*
>
> *After an Acquired Brain Injury, or ABI, the person sometimes remains in the life stage they were in at the time of the injury. In Gavin's case this was just after his twentieth birthday. He lived at home, and therefore he had no need to think about diet, shopping, cleaning, cooking and other such practical issues of daily living. So now he needs extra help to*

think about these things and to be reminded that they need to be seen to, and why.

- *Dis-inhibition: we have all learned to behave in a socially acceptable way and to use socially acceptable language. A brain injury can strip away all this socially learned behaviour and language, e.g. the need to close the bathroom door when using it. It can also lead to inappropriate behaviour – for instance, swearing or touching someone inappropriately.*
- *A brain injury can leave someone unable to be flexible in their thinking. If they want to do something, or have something done, in their mind there is only one way it should be done. If the person wants something done a particular way, they think it should be followed to the letter – and the fact that an able-bodied helper may not know or understand what is entailed is not accounted for or understood. Gavin is particularly inflexible about time. If a care shift is due to start at 9.00am he expects the care worker to be in by 9.00am – not 10 minutes later.*
- *It is up to us to take notice of these impairments and to discuss and negotiate and explain – for example, Gavin may not understand that the sun is shining but it is still December, and although it is warm in the house it is cold outside and coats must be worn. This is particularly important for Gavin – when his right side gets colder he experiences more pain.*

Wendy

Wendy also wrote some notes for the employed carers who come into Gavin's home to help him with the practical home tasks in his daily life:

He is paralysed down his right side. He is always in pain on this side of his body, especially in his hand and arm. This is made worse by being cold. He is epileptic.

Gavin is dysphasic – he knows what he want to say but cannot find the words. His memory is poor – one of his coping mechanisms is to call everyone by the same name or to add some sort of mnemonic as a reminder, e.g. Wendy-bendy. He is also mildly dyspraxic – he knows what he wants to do but the signals from his brain aren't relayed affectively. This is why he has difficulty in writing and can be quite clumsy. He also has acquired dyslexia.

Gavin is registered as partially sighted; he has no vision on his right side and his field of vision on the left side is limited. He also has some hearing loss on his right side. Therefore he prefers people to be on his left. Gavin has difficulty at times in coping with loud noises – this includes people speaking too loudly, or trying to follow conversations where there are several contributors, e.g. in a group such as a review meeting.

Speak to him face to face – do not call out from another room.

Gavin needs time to think about things and to respond to situations. Give him plenty of time to think about practical issues / activities, e.g. having a shower, keeping appointments, shopping, meal times. Plan these with him.

Staff withdraw, unless invited to stay, when he has visitors.

Gavin's disabilities can lead to people treating him like a child, or with undue familiarity. This is behaviour he recognises even if he cannot find the language to correct it – he must be treated with respect, and his rights and individuality recognised.

Be sensitive to and aware that you are in Gavin's home. Do not chivvy or hassle him. If the situation is getting out of control, or if Gavin tells you to, leave.

Means of communication in Gavin's home

The communications book is kept on the desk in the spare room. This should be used as a means of exchanging information between all who support Gavin. It is best to check this daily. Also there are the notice boards in the kitchen for urgent information, and of course the fridge door, especially for shopping lists – there is a fridge magnet to hold messages in place and the calendar for writing in appointments etc.

More general areas

• Trust Gavin's instinctive feelings / judgements about people.

- *Help Gavin do what he can't, e.g. money management, household decisions such as what to do about broken / malfunctioning equipment.*
- *Emergencies such as break-ins – Gavin doesn't have the language to say that he needs his mother / family. The consequence of this can be giving a care worker a hard time.*
- *Information processing – slow but it does happen.*
- *Help with coping in groups / crowds.*
- *Help with personal hygiene, prompting about having showers – which he will need assistance with – and changing clothes.*
- *Encouraging Gavin to have creams for psoriasis applied.*

Help with food shopping

A great team effort! But this couldn't happen without collaboration, co-ordination and effective communication between everyone involved, whether family or other informal home carers and professionals. All of this gives Gavin the daily support he needs, and means he can live independently as he wishes.

Whatever the condition, *whatever* the logistics involved, collaboration, good communication and co-ordination of care are essential to the best outcome for the individual at the centre of all our efforts. Thankfully, as we've seen, resources and approaches are changing. Without such collaboration, communication and co-ordination, any 'care plan' will inevitably be fragmented and patchy. Perhaps in reading this brief outline of changes in treatment approaches you can identify some of them in your own or your family's experiences past and present.

Notes

1 Hutchinson, G. and Hickling, F. (1999) *Problems in society, problems in psychiatry.* International Review of Psychiatry, 11: 162-7.
2 Whitaker, R. (2002, revised edition 2010) *Mad in America: Bad Science, Bad Medicine, and the Enduring Mistreatment of the Mentally Ill.* Basic Books, USA.
3 Levitt, S. D. and Dubner, S. J. (2005) *Freakonomics.* Penguin Books, UK.
4 *Guardian* newspaper, 17.2.06. www.theguardian.com (Accessed on 15/5/2014).
5 *Readers Digest*, January 2007 – quote from Sally Shannon.
6 *Readers Digest*, January 2007 – quote from Heller an Shapiro.
7 www.open.ac.uk/health-and-social-care (Accessed on 15/5/2014).
8 Schmidt, U., Treasure, J., Williams, C. and McCloskey, C. (2007) *Anorexia Nervosa: Effective Caring.* CD-Rom for Professionals and Carers. Media Innovations.
9 Mueser, K. T. and Gingerich, S. (1994) *Coping with Schizophrenia.* New Harbinger Publication, USA.
10 Read, J., Mosher, L. R. and Benstall, R. (Eds) (2004) *Models of Madness: Psychological, Social and Biological Approaches to Schizophrenia.* Brunner-Routledge.
11 *The Independent*, 08.04.05 (Accessed on 15/5/2014).
12 Geddes, J., Price, J. and McKnight, R. (Eds) (2012) *Psychiatry* (4th Edition). Oxford University Press.
13 Slade, M. (2009) *Personal Recovery and Mental Illness.* Cambridge University Press, UK.

14 www.rethink.org (Accessed on 15/5/2014).

15 www.yale.edu.PRCH (Accessed on 15/5/2014).

16 Treasure, J., Schmidt, U. and Macdonald, P. (2010) *The Clinician's Guide to Collaborative Caring in Eating Disorders: The new Maudsley method.* Routledge.

17 Slade, M. (2009) *Personal Recovery and Mental Illness.* Cambridge University Press.

18 Treasure, J., Schmidt, U. and Macdonald, P. (2010) *The Clinician's Guide to Collaborative Caring in Eating Disorders: The new Maudsley method.* Routledge.

19 Treasure, J., Smith, G. and Crane, A. (2007) *Skills-based Caring for a Loved One with an Eating Disorder.* Routledge.

4

Challenging Behaviour

What is 'Challenging Behaviour'?

Behaviours of such intensity and frequency that the physical safety of the person or others is likely to be placed in jeopardy, or behaviour which is likely to seriously limit or delay access to and use of ordinary community services.[1]

How does this fit with your own definition of 'challenging behaviour'? What of aggression towards others? Refusal to follow instructions, rules or guidelines? What of an individual's aggression towards themselves, head-banging, cutting, scratching, biting... Many people would find trying to cope with such a situation extremely challenging to their own peace of mind, and in each situation there will be very individual triggers for the behaviour others find challenging.

Individual backgrounds and reactions? Possible triggers?

Whatever circumstances a child is born into and encounters, childhood and growing up usually involve meeting and exploring (or perhaps avoiding) all sorts of experiences and situations, finding out what reactions and results and consequences there might be. Depending on all sorts of factors, e.g. genetic makeup, home and other experiences – from laissez-faire and complete freedom to very strict rules and expectations, or perhaps incomprehensible swings between these two extremes – individuals will react in a wide variety of ways. From love and fun and lots of support, to extremely difficult or even wretched experiences within the home – plus their experience of the world and people (inevitably also very varied) outside their own front door – children will bring a range of feelings and attitudes to any new, or known, person, group, situation or circumstance they meet. In their continuing explorations children will sometimes break boundaries, accidentally or deliberately, which may be interpreted by others as 'challenging behaviour'.

In *any* household it is usual that members are affected by the behaviour of everyone else. However, often it is only when things go wrong that we become aware of the extent to which someone else's routines, habits, likes and dislikes, feelings and moods, ways of self-expression, all affect our own lives and feelings, in ways that might otherwise go unremarked. And as always, different people may react in very different ways: some will try to protect the vulnerable person in every possible way – remember 'Kangaroo'? And 'Ostrich', with head stuck firmly in the sand (or glued to the TV)? What of 'Rhino' and the other recognisable personality approaches?

Each of us express our feelings in different ways – some of which may seem 'challenging' in some way to some other individuals.

Not *all* long-term mental health conditions, and conditions often referred to as 'learning difficulties' or 'learning disabilities', involve what may be called 'challenging behaviour'. Not *all* people with long-term physical conditions which involve losing the ability to do everyday tasks express their frustration verbally in an unpleasant or 'challenging' way. However, from my own experience, from listening to all the people I've interviewed, and from all the reading and research I've done, I know that many real-life stories do indeed involve really challenging situations and behaviour and frequently affect many lives. It was only after I met Alexis that I realised I'd been bracing myself to hear another such story.

I've never been given a diagnosis for Marisa – she's 24 now – I was eventually just told she has 'severe learning difficulties'. She was 15 days late. She wasn't a difficult birth, quite straightforward, but the cord was round her neck and she was very cold. She was a very 'good baby', liked her sleep – still does.

When my son was born, I realised gradually that Marisa wasn't responding as expected – she was happy to let others do everything for her, where her brother wanted to do everything for himself.

She was assessed at the Aberdeen Raeden Centre when she was 2, then went to an ordinary nursery, later on to the Anna Ritchie school where she did the rest of her schooling until she was 19.

Now? She wears two hearing aids, attends the Willow-bank day care centre in Peterhead, makes jams and chutney ... she's very content, very sociable, loves the routine. And everyone loves her. She comes to lots of things with us, everyone asks her to dance at events – everyone encourages her to try things. We're so lucky – our whole family and our neighbours help whenever needed, like when we need a babysitter. And we get 'respite care' one night a month, though it feels so strange without her, especially in the morning and not sending her off to school.

When she was 16 we became her legal guardians, for decisions when Marisa couldn't do it – for instance, if she needed an operation. And we're making a will to make sure our daughter has the right care afterwards – it's important to make plans for all eventualities.

I know how lucky I am – I've heard lots of stories from other folk, and not everyone can cope when things are difficult. There's no training for family carers either, they're just expected to cope.

Alexis, interview

Alexis, Marisa and their family's story – an exception? Sadly, in addition to the exhaustion of being 'on call' 24 hours of every day, many home carers really struggle to cope with behaviour they find extremely difficult. This can challenge not only their peace of mind and home life, but it may also destroy their memories of their loved one, challenging their beliefs of what is acceptable behaviour and what they can reasonably cope with. Few family members and close friends, most especially when sharing a household, will remain unaffected.

Just a few examples of 'challenging behaviour':

- frequent unpredictable extreme rages over trivia
- hostility and rejection of attempts to help
- rudeness and physical or verbal aggression

- manipulation of others, playing one against another
- threats (e.g. of suicide or running away) if someone says *No* or the individual does not get their own way
- repeated unpleasant personal remarks designed to annoy and upset
- denial of actions, e.g. stealing money to fund bingeing, whether alcohol, eating, gambling or drugs
- shouting, screaming, slamming doors
- accusations of others 'not understanding'
- self-harm.

Perhaps you recognise some of these in your own home situation?

Practical activity

Read again the beginning of the chapter.
Read the questions and notes.
Discuss the questions below with your home team, self help group or group of friends.

Individual interpretations? Some people seem to ignore what others find very rude, off-putting, offensive or frightening. Or perhaps they may condemn certain behaviour while accepting, or even ignoring, similar behaviour in other people.

- Is it right at any time to simply ignore difficult behaviour in the hope it won't be repeated? Or to ignore and find excuses for it? If so, in what circumstances?
- When there are unforeseen consequences for the troubled person and/or others, even possibly legal or court action – how much should situation and the background to the incident be taken into account?
- To what extent should a person's individual difficulties be taken into account – for instance, personal stress, lack of understanding of what is unacceptable behaviour to others and its consequences, distorted thinking at the time, mental health problems?

So many questions, so many factors!

First steps

Whatever the situation, *whoever* has been in any way involved, a first step to deciding action (or perhaps simply taking note for the future) is to try to find out exactly what has happened, and why. If at all possible, talk to everyone involved. This may mean listening and keeping calm when others are upset or angry – not easy.

Inevitably individual views of events, and responses to them, will differ not only in terms of what an individual remembers but also in their personal interpretations.

Truth or lies?

In any situation called Trouble, some children – and adults – tell their version of the truth. Some 'miss out' any of their actions which didn't show them in a good light, and others simply deny their part completely. *Therefore it is very important to talk separately to each person involved in any incident, noting similarities in the stories – and any differences. Then get everyone involved together, and talk through what you've learned – stressing that because you're puzzled by the differences in the stories, you'd like to work out what really happened.*

I've also worked with some children who were at all times disconcertingly honest about their behaviour – though no experience can compare with the most startling example I've ever come across:

> *'Let me go!' she screams, thrashing against me. I lie next to her, holding her arms down. 'If you tell me you won't try to hurt Bodhi, I can let you go,' I tell her.*
> *'I have to hurt Bodhi!' she screams.*
> *'You may feel you have to, but you don't.'*
> *'I do have to … I want to.'*
> From an edited extract in *Guardian* weekend, 19.01.13, from Michael Schofield's 'January First: A Child's Descent into Madness And Her Father's Struggle to Save Her',[2] which tells the harrowing story of his daughter Janni's high intelligence, her frequent violence towards her brother and her hallucinations from an early age, until her diagnosis of child-onset schizophrenia.

Thankfully such an extreme story, and diagnosis, is rare.

With some conditions, for instance in some compulsive/addictive conditions, family members may suspect – even have proof – that someone is inventing a very different version to what everyone else has seen, heard or experienced, and that person may even believe in their own self-deception when they blame others. However, unless everyone in the household sits down together often and discusses their observations, frequently the individual at the centre will be able to continue with their own self-destruction while at the same time destroying the family, and further hasten their own self-destructive downward spiral in the process.

> *I've lost my job now because I was taking money out of the safe, that's how bad it's got. At first I always managed to replace it ... but then the gambling took over. I've borrowed from family, from friends, I use credit cards and even high-interest payday loans ... I've got really good at lying, I even begin to believe myself ... things like, the car's broken down, I can't get to work, or the home improvements have cost more than expected ... always I think the next bet will pay off the debt, the mortgage, whatever. Just now I reckon I'm about £15,000 in debt. And my wife knows now, says she'll leave if I don't sort things out ... so far I've always managed to talk her out of it.*
>
> R, personal contact

Perhaps you can imagine some of the scenes in R's house. While R has now recognised the effects of his behaviour on his family, and has sought help through Gamblers Anonymous, for a wide variety of reasons in other situations there may be no such recognition.

In your own situation ... can you identify possible trigger factors? Could the challenging behaviour be due to:

- *fear of change*: of the unknown; of being wrong; of being unable to cope; of deteriorating faculties; of loss of control; of being unable to understand; of feeling under threat; of being abandoned?

- *frustration*: at change of routine; at being unable to do something; at being unable to understand something; or being unable to find the right words?
- *feelings of loss of control?*
- *unexpected change of routine?*
- *lack of understanding of what's happening?*
- *heightened reaction*: to sound, light, materials, physical sensations such as feeling constricted by hat and scarf?
- *temptation and compulsive habit*: accessibility of drink, money to gamble or feed another addiction?

Perhaps a combination of trigger factors?

Anxiety may also apply to any of the factors above – and sometimes several factors combine, e.g. someone feels nervous in a particular situation, worried they can't cope, and extremely frustrated that they don't have the words to explain how they feel.

Careful observation is an important key

Remember – as with everything else in human beings, emotional reactions are very individual. What may seem absolutely trivial to you can trigger an extreme reaction in someone else. Try to keep an open mind in trying to identify triggers for behaviour.

Perhaps you and your home team, close contacts too, can identify some of the behaviours you're coping with and work out possible triggers? Using the list above, try to work out possible triggers to the challenging behaviour you recognise in your own situation.

Practical activity

Think of someone you know who reacts with 'challenging' behaviour. Can you think of factors which trigger the difficult behaviour? Perhaps a recurring situation?

Keep a brief record of WHEN (date, time) and WHERE (place, situation) challenging behaviour occurs. WHAT happens? Note also any important factors or events which took place just before the extreme reaction. Can you identify a pattern? A common factor which leads to the unpleasant behaviour? For instance, where any addictive/compulsive behaviours are involved and these have led to distorted thinking, some people may be simply annoying, others aggressive and spoiling for a fight with anyone who crosses their path. There is little point in trying to discuss an individual's behaviour with them at this time – let them argue with themselves, better to wait until the anti-social behaviour has worn off before even attempting to discuss their behaviour and its effects on yourself and others.

If it's possible to identify a particular situation which regularly leads to unpleasant and unacceptable behaviour, it may then be possible to work out ways of avoiding the situation altogether. If this is not a possibility, perhaps help and encourage and support the individual to cope better in the situation. For example, if someone has an extreme reaction to the sound of a vacuum cleaner, is it possible for Hoovering to be done while that individual is out? Or where a particular material causes extreme discomfort, perhaps avoid buying clothes made of that material?

Sometimes a fierce temper and a lack of patience is part of a person's genetic makeup, or perhaps emotional distress always occurs in certain situations. Brain injury or particularly traumatic experiences can also lead to dramatic changes in personality. Any disability may mean intense frustration for an individual, while in dementia, for example, a loss of being able to make sense of the world may lead at times to unexpected conclusions. For instance, when my mother developed Alzheimer's, at times she was very rude to long-time friends and others who had helped her. Sometimes she didn't recognise relatives and close friends, yet this caused no upset at all to her. On other occasions when she didn't recognise a family member or friend, she wouldn't believe the answer – and got very angry with everyone round her, accusing them of lying to her. One day I visited her:

GS *Hello, mother.*
MOTHER *Hello, dear. How are you?*
GS *Fine, mother.*
MOTHER *And how's your daughter?*
(*Wonderful,* I thought, *this is a really good day, she remembers her grand-daughter!*)
GS *Fine, mother.*

MOTHER *And how's your son?*
GS *Fine, mother.*
MOTHER *And how's your sister?*
GS *Fine, mother.*
MOTHER *And how's your mother?*

Is routine important?

For anyone on the autistic spectrum, routine and regular patterns are especially important, and even the smallest change can bring an extreme reaction.

> *Class 6 was told that Maths was first that Wednesday, followed by Language work, and then after break they'd get changed for Physical Education, all written up on the board under 'Plan for Today'. The class settled to Maths – then a message came to say the PE timetable had been changed, and their class should get ready immediately for PE.*
>
> *Most of the children were delighted – but H went into a screaming rage at being disturbed from his Maths calculations.*
>
> AN

Keeping a record, with dates, times etc., no matter how brief, may not only be useful in identifying the frequency of these incidents. It may also give a clue about possible triggers – for instance, eating a particular food. Some foods and drinks have been banned due to the use of a chemical which can cause an adverse reaction in behaviour.

> *Within just a few minutes at the party, A, aged 7, seemed to change completely from happy and laughing as he joined in the games, to running wildly round the hall, yelling and screaming, hitting out at any one who came near or was in his way. Having known A for almost 3 years, the change was quite a shock. When A's mother was contacted, her immediate question was 'I've noticed that he reacts badly when he's been drinking diluted orange juice – has he had any?'*
>
> *Yes, he had. And when his mother arrived, A refused to get in the car to take him home, kicked and screamed and fought.*
>
> NL

Keeping notes is not only useful in identifying possible patterns; they can also be useful in offering information to treating professionals, who may find it hard to reconcile the calm and often charming individual sitting in front of them in the structured environment of an office or clinic with home carers' descriptions of their behaviour at other times – see Jane Gregory's *Bringing Up a Challenging Child at Home: Where Love is Not Enough*[3] – and once patterns can be identified, it may be possible to find ways to intercept and change those patterns.

With A, being sure to avoid eating or drinking anything containing tartrazine[4] – also known as additive E102, C.I. 19140, or FD&C Yellow 5 – made a huge difference (see also Chapter 6).

For C, wearing loose clothes which did not rub or constrict led to her feeling much more relaxed and comfortable, and happier with the world and herself.

With L, the family made sure that any noisy machines, e.g. Hoovers, spin driers etc., were used only when L wasn't at home.

It's wonderful to know many children – and adults – who have had major difficulties and needed extra support in all sorts of ways, but have recognised their problems, tackled them and worked out what they needed – may still need – and have overcome their former negative patterns to emerge much stronger and able to cope.

Calm and consistent – and finding the right words

When someone is having a 'Hairy Jamaica' – my daughter's much-later description of her/anorexia's extreme rages over trivia when she was ill – it is very difficult to keep calm when you yourself are the butt of all the extreme behaviour. Even when you know that reacting in a similar way means that the situation is most likely to become even further inflamed, finding the right words to try to calm the situation can be very difficult.

Therefore it can be very useful to work out in advance what needs to be said in recurring situations; words you can repeat as necessary, such as:

No! – shouting, screaming, biting, swearing, kicking, hitting is not acceptable. No! I will not accept this. Shouting, screaming, biting, kicking, hitting is not acceptable. No! I don't like it when you ... I don't accept it from anyone else, and I won't accept it from you. No! I don't like it and I won't accept it.

When someone is out of control, better not to try to reason – simply try to contain. If the person is not in any danger, keep repeating your chosen words until you feel you can withdraw: *Now I'm going to leave you and –* for example *– walk the dog; wash the dishes; make the tea; work in the garden, the garage, the kitchen... We'll talk about this when you are calm.*

Whatever the definition or circumstances, and the reasons for the behaviour or the consequences, challenging behaviour can often mean that the troubled individual will not reach his or her full potential in many areas of life. As we've seen, each individual and their situation will be different depending on a wide variety of factors. *Whatever* the reason for the behaviour presenting the challenge, whether it is due to lack of understanding or frustration because of a life-affecting disability, or a mental health problem after some sort of intense personal stress, or an addiction, or a myriad of other possible explanations – finding the key to the personal stress, anxiety or discomfort and working out a way of easing it can mean a huge difference all round, both in the moment and for the future.

No easy answers, and unfortunately I have no magic wand; despite searching far and wide over many years, so far I haven't found the right catalogue... I wish it could be that easy! However, from my own experiences and listening to those of many others, I've suggested some steps that home carers can try which may help change or reduce the distressing effects of very difficult and challenging reactions. I hope these will help you find practical ideas to work out the best approaches in your own situation.

Notes

1 Emerson, E. and Einfeld, S. (1987) *Challenging Behaviour.* Cambridge University Press.

2 Schofield, M. (2013) *January First: A Child's Descent into Madness and Her Father's Struggle to Save Her.* Hardie Grant Books, Australia.
3 Gregory, J. (2000) *Bringing Up a Challenging Child at Home: Where Love is Not Enough.* Jessica Kingsley.
4 www.ukfoodguide.net (Accessed on 15/5/2014).

5

Family Teamwork
How?

Teams can produce a quality and quantity of work far higher than the sum of what the separate individuals could have produced on their own.

R Meredith Belbin[1]

Although Belbin was writing about business, the same is true in so many other situations. Without teamwork, without any co-ordination of effort, collaboration and effective communication, lacking relevant information and resources, and even with everyone doing their very best, it is very unlikely that the results will be as effective as they could be.

But – what is 'a team'? According to Chambers' Thesaurus[2], pseudonyms of team include: band; group; line-up; gang; squad; crew; troupe. And pseudonyms for teamwork? Collaboration; co-operation; co-ordination; esprit de corps; fellowship; joint effort; team spirit.

And – what makes 'a team'?

In sport individuals will be selected for physical fitness and outstanding co-ordination; in an orchestra or music group they will be selected for particular talent and skill; in a quiz situation for their knowledge of particular subjects and a good memory. In any recognised 'team' of people, in a work or voluntary situation, there is usually also a recognised list of required, expected or hoped-for characteristics and training.

Practical activity

Think of your own family and other families you know. What would your definition of 'family' be? If possible, discuss with family and/or friends – do you all have the same definition?

Whether or not there is a blood, ancestral or legally-binding relationship, families are made up of individuals who happen to share accommodation and certain bonds, perhaps through marriage, blood relationships, or past and/or current experiences. They may also share some recognisable personality traits, which may affect relationships within the group at any time.

In a work situation people are appointed for their ability and qualifications, which may be extremely narrow and very specialised or widely varied and involving a broad spectrum of required abilities, ranging from technical skill to joinery to cooking to teaching to admin to computer and website work ... the list of jobs in today's world is endless.

But none of these abilities, skills, talents and qualifications mean that these individual people – even someone with a long list of relevant qualifications and experience – will definitely prove to be a good, reliable and effective team member.

So ... what hope for building teamwork in a family? In a family there's no question of initial selection, no assessment, no audition or interview, let alone any training. There are no recognised qualifications to be part of any family, no internationally accepted rule book to be noted and quoted. Depending on a huge range of factors, every family is different and each family has to find its own way.

As in *any* team, *any* task or project, when all is going well, it is only too easy not to notice the individual efforts – and the organisation and teamwork underlying that smooth surface. Also, it is only too easy to recognise when things go badly wrong and disintegrate into chaos – and then into ongoing bad feeling, personal animosity and recriminations, all of which, if ignored, can spell disaster for whatever project 'the team' has been involved in. Can the same be said of a 'family team', most especially during 'tough times'?

An impossible dream?

Is the idea of a family, made up of individuals of all ages, all stages, working as a support team even possible? Or is it simply an impossible dream? Think of a few you know personally. *Can a family group build such a dream, work as a team in creating effective support, provide that essential care 24 hours a day, 365 days a year?*

I believe that with love and much goodwill, the answer is *yes!*

How?

Jamie Sams and David Carson put it this way:

> In building a dream, teamwork is necessary. To accomplish a goal with others involves working with the group mind.
>
> From *Medicine Cards* (1988).[3]

Usually in maths and science a formula can be found which, when applied to a defined problem in a logical way, will solve that problem. However, even here it is possible that unexpected snags arise: new information may come to light, research published on what is found to be flawed information; misprints may trip up the mathematicians, the theorists, the researchers and scientists who think they have found the answer to any particular problem.

Have you ever tried to apply logic, any formula, to human beings, to families of all shapes and sizes, ages and stages?

A different kind of family?

Ken Milroy has worked with Aberdeen Foyer since its beginning in 1995, supporting young homeless people and helping them towards supporting themselves through good self-care including diet, healthy living and exercise, confidence-building and motivation, giving them support and practical experience to prepare them for life outside a home situation. When asked about building a team from scratch, he answered:

Knitting the family...

I believe that real teamwork is based on having a common
purpose, having shared values, and it's like active learning
– an ongoing process. In a business, it's like 'taking the
temperature' of the company. And we have to structure what
we've learned. Writing down what we learn is useful – and
making sure that everyone knows what's going on.

Make sure everyone feels valued – at work that means
the secretary, the janitor as well as the managers. Give
people opportunities, it's like investing in people. Make sure
they don't feel isolated – don't operate in a bubble, get out
there and talk to folk about what they're doing, how they
feel, what they think. Leadership is more important than
'management'.

What is a leader? A leader is a good listener, a good communicator, able to motivate and inspire, live your values – 'walk the walk, talk the talk'. Wherever possible, lead from the front, through involving people and giving them feedback.

Language is really important – We instead of I.

Take a step at a time, check and reflect.

The organisation isn't me, it's everyone in the team.

The pitfalls? People not pulling their weight, lack of information and relevant training.

> Ken Milroy, Aberdeen Foyer, interview

Along the way, to help give work experience in a supportive situation, Aberdeen Foyer has set up and developed from scratch two restaurants, a graphic design business, a property maintenance company and a driving company, all of which provide support, practical training and experience for young homeless people who lack or have lost such structure and support – before they move on to make their own way in the 'outside world'.

A different kind of family? Yes – and with the same ultimate goals of providing support, guidance, experience in life skills such as healthy diet and exercise, and a great deal of caring until someone is strong enough to be able to follow their own independent path.

Practical activity

If possible, share and discuss with a partner, friend or group.

- Think of a situation you know well – home, work, sport, social, choir, or somewhere else – where teamwork is needed.
- Make a list of what *you* think is essential to make that team effective, e.g. information, resources. What information, what resources? And what else?
- What strengths can you recognise that are already there?
- Are there any qualities you feel are missing or that need more development?
- Discuss your ideas with a colleague or friend – have they identified the same strengths and possible weaknesses?
- Review your initial list of qualities required – is there anything you want to change?

- Are the same qualities needed in every team? Or are there differences depending on situations and people?

It often seems easy to recognise *a lack of* teamwork and *a lack of* 'team spirit' – though it is sometimes difficult to identify what exactly turns a particular group of individuals into an active and really effective team who focus on a common aim, supporting each other through thick and thin and personal exhaustion to bring about that common aim.

Over when and where we are born, and into which individual family, we have no choice. Yet when they are presented with really tough times, many families composed of very different ages, stages and personalities, with a huge range of individual needs, interests, energy, abilities and approaches – as well as weaknesses – can indeed somehow develop into effective support teams. I've met several.

Although relevant information, ability, personal skills, talents and possibly training and motivation can all be important, *any* good team depends on the ability of the team members to work together. As Ken Milroy says, this involves many skills – the ability to share information, knowledge and skills, the ability to develop and build on that combined knowledge and those skills, and the ability to co-ordinate efforts towards the agreed goal. This may take many forms: to win a particular game; to sell more articles to gain a larger bonus; to teach a co-ordinated curriculum from early stages through to mature writing, reading and use of maths and science, reaching 'targets' at various stages; to train in readiness to take responsibility and independence; to perform complicated life-saving operations where each team member has to be in tune with and react well at the right times ... or to successfully treat, nurse back to health, help and support someone to reach their full potential or regain their former strength and abilities in life.

Whatever the goal, ideally aims will be discussed and agreed with everyone in the team who contributes to the recognised joint effort.

Ideally, yes – but rarely do ideal circumstances exist, either in work or voluntary situations and let alone in a home team struggling with very tough times and trying to work out what to do when coping with unforeseen circumstances which may

– and often do – include difficult and challenging behaviour from a loved one.

Constructive teambuilding – rules

In any work team or charity, social or other established group, there will be agreed rules, often written down although possibly not always agreed by the people originally involved. The rules may have been drawn up at some point in the past, quite possibly in different circumstances which don't take various more-recent factors into account; it is unfortunately all too easy for daily routines to become thoughtless habits which may continue long after their usefulness has expired. Therefore outlining, discussing and reviewing 'the rules and routines' can be a very fruitful exercise in identifying out-moded habits and finding things that might work better in revised circumstances.

This is true even with a group of people with a common interest, willingness and ability who have similar or complementary qualifications. It is even more the case when a co-ordinated approach is needed in a much more informal, fluid and quite possibly challenging situation.

And in a family? Given a wide variety of ages from young children upwards, different experiences, viewpoints and ways of self-expression, quite possibly involving some past or current disagreements and heated arguments which may become even more likely while living through tough times when relationships may become fraught – is this an impossible task? *All* families go through tough times: parents don't always agree, siblings often argue and fall out, people may be worried about money, work/homework, exams, about a relationship or life in general. A small irritation may explode into a major catastrophe which everyone sees from their own unique perspective. As Ross W Greene states, '*Add an explosive child to the mix, and you'll push many families and marriages to the brink*'.[4]

An explosive child (or an older person?) who gets easily frustrated, finds it difficult or even impossible to be flexible and to consider problems rationally or see different options and ways forward? Yes, a child who finds even minor changes impossible to cope with may indeed bring a family to breaking point. The same can happen in *any* family situation, where a loved one of *any* age needs extra time, care, support and attention, all while day-to-day life activities still need to continue for all the other members. The physical and emotional strain of offering extra ongoing support will inevitably have effects on everyone.

Perhaps relevant professional experience helps prepare for personal experience?

Despite all my training, and years of work experience in mental health, I was totally unprepared for the effects on our family when my son developed schizophrenia.

I, psychiatrist, personal contact

Even with my training and many years of experience working with children and families, I too felt totally unprepared to struggle without information about the illness, and totally powerless to help my daughter when she changed from a 'Tigger' figure to showing sudden extreme screaming rages, not accepting she was ill and refusing treatment. It took me a long time to work out what not to do, what definitely didn't help, and what might – just might – really help my beloved Jay.

The next quote comes from an interview in the *Radio Times*, 3–9 April 2010.[5] The presenter introduced Professor Martin Elliott, one of the UK's leading cardiothoracic surgeons who performs two to three hundred operations a year on children at London's Great Ormond Street Hospital, and described how he recognised his huge responsibilities with cases so complex that often other hospitals felt unable to accept them. Speaking of his work, Professor Elliott emphasised that teamwork forms 'the backdrop' against which all other decisions take place – he could not undertake such work without an effective team.

Key among his duties is managing the expectations of desperate parents. Professor Elliott understands that while it's difficult enough for doctors to wrestle with the ethical issues presented by their young patients, it's far harder for parents trying to juggle complicated medical data alongside the inevitable maelstrom of emotions engendered by caring for a sick child.

Speaking of his own son Toby's death aged 26, subsequently discovered to be due to sudden death in epilepsy, Professor

Elliott said, *'I was just completely unprepared for it. You cease to be rational, and if the families are anything like I felt, then you're just exhausted. It consumes you, and your decision-making is all over the place.'*

Co-ordination of effort may be a huge task within *any* team whatever the situation, whether family or professional team, or a mix of family and professionals – and the more people there are involved, the more important effective communication, collaboration, and co-ordination become. This is even more true when several teams of professionals are involved, possibly with bases a distance apart, as well as informal home care givers, all involved in building that crucial support and care – which is well worth all the effort.

There are so many projects and tasks in life where co-ordination and teamwork are important ... and libraries and bookshops can often offer whole shelves of books on Teamwork and Leadership, some quoting research on these subjects in business situations. Committees, Task Forces, Quality Circles and Project Groups are named as types of groups which can become close-knit teams 'with the right sort of leader'.

My mum and dad have been married for almost forever ... and we all live quite near. I don't really know who would be 'leader'. We've always sort of talked a lot – and argued! – then somehow it just happens. We always had to take our turn to do chores, sort of share things out. I still really hate my turn for cleaning the bathroom! Maybe it's not possible to have a leader in a family.

M

What do you think?

In situations great and small

Teamwork, with perseverance and long-term commitment, calm and consistent efforts plus the other basic Cs – co-ordination, cooperation, collaboration, constructive communication – can lead to huge positive changes in situations great and small. Here is just one example:

Despite the efforts over many years of Dr Harry Millar and a few other professionals to build more appropriate and effective specialist NHS inpatient care in Scotland for eating disordered patients in a life-threatening condition, it was only when a small group of family carers started a petition about the situation and presented it to the Scottish Petitions Committee ... who passed it on to the Scottish Health Committee ... who organised a public enquiry about the situation, with presentations from Dr Millar and other professionals as well as from family members ... that real change began to happen, leading to the current much more co-ordinated service across Scotland with its many scattered and rural communities.

After a three-year campaign, Managed Clinical Networks were set up in 2005 with groups of professionals representing services in groups of hospitals and making decisions for groups of regions working together – e.g. Tayside, Highland and Grampian, where a specialist NHS inpatient ward in Aberdeen, the first in Scotland, serves all three areas, meaning that patients (often in life-threatening conditions) do not have to travel hundreds of miles south for inpatient treatment. It also means that it is easier to preserve continuity in a patient's life through family and friends being able to visit.

Now, rather than each hospital and its staff working in isolation, information and resources are pooled and co-ordinated – *but none of this could have happened had it not been for the team efforts of everyone involved, both home carers and professionals.*

Think of your own situation, or those of friends. Do they feel part of a home team? No? What needs to change? And how? Can every family member be an effective team player? What about Great Aunt Jemima, who is always sure she is absolutely right in all circumstances and will carry on regardless? (Some say she was simply born awkward...)

The realistic answer is *NO* – but most members of most families want to help their fellow members, want to do their very best for them, want to help in tough times if they possibly can. Most welcome the opportunity of discussion to learn what their vulnerable loved one needs.

Note the word *most*. For an infinite number of reasons, not every single family member can play the same equally supportive role. For instance, perhaps Great Aunt Jemima is too set in her ways to take on board what for her would be a major change in approach – in her day, if someone didn't 'toe the line' or was out of order in the behaviour department, there were immediate and serious sanctions. Great Aunt Jemima recognises only her own 'line', and expects everyone else to do so too.

As Stephen R Covey states in *The 7 Habits of Highly Effective Families*,[6] *'People don't see the world as it is: they see it as they are – or as they are conditioned to be.'*

In other words, individuals perceive the world in their own particular way – whether due to their 'conditioning', or their own mix of genes and life experience (nature and nurture, or an individual mix of both) – and they assume that their view of the world is right. Just ask three people who were present at the same event for their account of that event. Do they all focus on the same aspects, see the same things, remember the same sequence? Feel the same about what has happened?

With home carers now being recognised as playing an important part in building the most effective all-round care and support, do families commonly see themselves as a team? For instance, see *Proactive, Planned and Coordinated: Care Management in Scotland*[7] – or look for a similar document related to your own location. If not, how can families build towards this goal?

First step – communication

Without everyone sitting down together, misunderstandings are likely to flourish and grow. *Therefore, if at all possible get everyone in the household together to discuss their own observations and feelings.* If anyone says they see no need for such a meeting or there is no need for them to be there, no-one can force them to be present. Simply state that if they're not there, anyone can say anything about them or their behaviour … and they won't be there to give their own point of view.

Set up a regular time for the family to meet as a group to discuss specific issues. Daily/weekly/fortnightly/monthly? Depending on what needs to be discussed, who needs to be there, and the urgency of the items under review, the home group can decide on what's needed. (No meeting needed, all going swimmingly, nothing to discuss? A celebration is surely in order!)

In work situations, this may be called a 'Staff Meeting' with a formal or more informal agenda to focus discussion. In a family this could be called a 'Family Forum', 'Round-the-Table Time', 'Talking Time' or 'Team Time'. Even a 'Home Huddle'? Perhaps someone might come up with an original name for your own home team meetings.

When?

It may be possible to plan for your own family discussions at a regular time, perhaps every week, or it may only be possible to fit them in on an ad hoc basis. The important thing is for *everyone* to feel that there will be a time when their concerns will be listened to and hopefully some sort of solution found.

When a time is agreed to suit as many as possible, this can mean that some family members might need to rearrange their schedule for work or school to enable them to attend – e.g. Dad might have to go in to work late and leave later, or Auntie might offer to babysit for the youngest member of the family, or perhaps brother or sister might skip going to gymnastics, or football, or choir practice.

Where?

Choose a place where everyone can feel as relaxed as possible – ask people where they think would be best to meet. When people suggest different possible meeting places, perhaps the venue could change from meeting to meeting? Depending on anticipated numbers:

- Round a table? In a kitchen or dining area? Or perhaps in a more formal setting?
- In the garden?
- Over coffee/juice and biscuits?
- After a meal together?
- Somewhere else?

Who should attend the meetings?

- As 'home team' members are usually the first to notice a change in behaviour, either negative or positive, if at all possible every member of the household should be there at regular review meetings.
- Everyone relevant to the care of the vulnerable individual at that point who can contribute to a review of the current situation, and – with 'home team' agreement – close friends and neighbours may also be included.
- Depending on the situation, the condition or illness, sometimes your vulnerable loved one will be able to attend. (Indeed, if they have previously been unaware of or unwilling to accept how their behaviour affects others in the household, they may *need* to hear how others feel – although they may not like or want to accept what they hear; see below.)
- Young carers – no matter how young, a child needs reassurance and an explanation at the right level when they are affected by changes in a loved one's mood and behaviour.

Peter, aged 6, his lip quivering – *Grandpa told me to get out of his way, I'm just a pest. He used to like doing LEGO with me, liked to take me to football, liked when we went to the river to feed the ducks... I don't know why he doesn't love me any more.*

Dad – *Grandpa isn't feeling very well just now, he feels very very tired and sometimes a bit cross and frustrated when his sore leg hurts and won't do what he wants it to do. And he can't get out golfing or walking now. Maybe you could get his book for him, or read the sports pages in his newspaper with him? What do you think, is there anything you can think of to help him?*

What if the problems are denied by the person at the centre of all these efforts?

For a multitude of reasons – perhaps a lack of understanding, a lack of relevant information on the 'whole picture' or reluctance to accept a diagnosis and possible prognosis – personal denial may play a part. Where any addictive/compulsive behaviours

Peter and Grandpa

are part of the problem, a denial of any personal responsibility is often the case. Frequently, family members sigh with relief on a relatively peaceful day (I know I did), and may avoid mentioning their own feelings – frustration, isolation, anger, grief, anxiety, despair – for fear of triggering more challenging behaviour and yet another difficult incident.

Although perhaps initially reluctant to attend, most people agree to take part in meetings – if only because they can't resist hearing what is being said, especially if they think it's about them. See also the chapter on *Communication*.

What's to be discussed?

- No matter how small any matter may seem, if someone has raised it, don't ignore or belittle whatever it is – if it matters to someone, it is affecting their life and their feelings.
- Try to include *any* instances of positive incidents – notice and praise the positive.
- Where necessary, reminders that different individuals may have different understandings and viewpoints, which in turn may lead to further constructive discussion.

Who will lead the meetings?

In a formal meeting usually one person leads the group, or 'takes the chair', to introduce discussions on a list of topics agreed before the meeting. Alternatively, perhaps several people take turns; there is no one 'Right Way'. In family meetings the same is true. After initial family discussion about who will lead the meetings, the leader:

- may be clear and agreed with little or no discussion – possibly mum or dad, or a grandparent
- may depend on many factors such as family structure, ages and stages
- may be a special family friend, a neighbour, or even a supportive professional who may be asked to help when strong individual feelings make the situation difficult
- may mostly be one person, with another 'standing in' as necessary
- may rotate, with each member taking a turn.

What does the 'chairperson' or leader do at each meeting?

- Welcome everyone and acknowledge efforts to be there.
- Talk about the rough agenda, and outline any items that are already known about. Ask for late additional topics that someone wants discussed urgently – or discuss whether this item may be noted for a later get-together (perhaps suggest a special extra meeting).

Rules

Introduce the idea that to help make sure everyone, of all ages, has the opportunity to talk about how they feel, rules are needed. (Rules may be changed or added to if/when the situation changes, or when it's recognised that something hasn't been noted before.)

Agree on the best start time, and say when you think the team meeting will end, so that others can then plan their follow-on activities, whether they are work, personal interests, hobbies or a favourite TV programme. Setting an end time can also encourage everyone to stick to the time limit.

No mobile phones, tablet computers, games or any other distractions. Discuss why family members and their welfare and well-being are *much* more important than any mechanical or internet game.

Try to encourage a calm atmosphere. If and when things get a bit heated, suggest a five-minute break.

Try to keep discussion to what was agreed before the meeting. If someone introduces a new topic, speaks about an incident or follows a different plan from the one already agreed, say that it'll be noted and discussed later; perhaps there will be time at the end of the current meeting, and if not it will be included in the next meeting.

Only one voice speaking at a time, with reminders as needed, to allow everyone to be heard and to make it easier for everyone to listen and discuss. This is especially important for anyone with hearing problems.

Try to ensure that no one person dominates the meeting. A maximum number of minutes for any person to speak should be discussed and agreed at the very first meeting – for instance a maximum of two or three minutes for any one contribution, which may be reviewed at a later date. By setting a limit, whatever it is, people will hopefully think about what they really want to say and come prepared, rather than blether on too much.

Appoint a timekeeper. To encourage everyone to keep within the agreed time limit for individual contributions, it's a good idea to have a timer, or timekeeper, and choose a signal for '*Stop, it's .....'s turn now!*' The signal can be anything that makes a noise – perhaps the oldest or the youngest family member could be asked to choose what to use. A treasured family gavel or other wooden item? Two LEGO pieces knocked together? A favourite rattle or squeaker? A triangle or other musical instrument? It doesn't really matter what is used; the important thing is that everyone knows and remembers the signal that time's up. If the rules about one voice at a time or time limits are broken and things get out of hand, that gavel, squeaker or rattle will come in very handy!

No interruptions when someone is talking. Remind anyone trying to interrupt that their turn will come – they must be patient, and when it's their own turn no-one will interrupt them.

Consider all suggestions. Asking for lots of ideas and possible solutions to tackle a given situation and making a list – sometimes called brainstorming – can be really helpful. Ideas may range from serious to funny and OTT (these ideas can often give a valuable lift to the mood of the meeting!).

Encourage exploration of different perspectives and the discussion of pros and cons. Before any decision is considered, *discuss* reasons why it might – or might not – be a good idea, and why.

Encourage younger people and quieter members. By referring to comments you've heard them make, or reminding them of significant incidents they might want to mention, try to include any naturally quiet, shy or nervous members.

Try to ensure that everyone has had opportunities to comment. Where there is disagreement, perhaps say *'We'll come back to this another time; let's see if we can all come up with some realistic ideas that could help'*. Be prepared to repeat this if and when necessary.

Discuss and set the date of the next meeting.

And the final question at every meeting: ask for any feedback about how people felt about the meeting and any particular outcomes, whether these were good or bad. This can be done using a sheet of paper with a happy face drawn at the top labelled 'Worked Well', for people to note what they felt was effective, and on the other side an unhappy face for comments on things they think you should 'Do Differently'.

Use this feedback to adjust arrangements for another time.

All participants: if possible, let the chairperson know in advance if you want something in particular (an incident or anything else) discussed, or else bring it up at the beginning of a meeting. A whiteboard in the kitchen can be very useful for this, where everyone is free to add suggestions when they think of them.

All these are suggestions to be discussed with the family team, adopted or adapted, reviewed and developed as needed. Are there any other rules that you think might be needed in your own situation?

Finally – everyone needs to be appreciated. VIEW – Very Important Encouraging Words – are always important, for *all* individual members of *any* team. *I really appreciate ... thanks for ... I noticed ...* Be sure to comment on anything positive, no matter how small. All too often we only comment when we notice things that are not to our liking!

Leading your home team

What qualities are needed for leadership? Are they the same in *any* team, whatever the circumstances or situation?

Practical activity

This can be done individually, or you could make it a group discussion and ask home team members what *they* think is important for their meetings.

Ask them to write down the qualities that are important to leading a good team at work.

A few thoughts of my own:

Clear view of main aims in the long term: expects the best, prepares for the worst; shares relevant information; appreciates strengths; recognises weaknesses (including his or her own); ability to listen; fairness; intuition, observation and awareness; able to remain calm under pressure and provocation; encourages debate; doesn't always think they have to know the answer.

Gives credit whenever possible: proactive; practical; positive; encourages self-preservation – look after each other; consistent; trusts their fellow team members to do their best; able to delegate; realises impact of own behaviour on others; appreciates differences and clarifies issues; deals with disagreements impartially; considers all available information and relevant factors; when necessary, addresses and deals with confrontation; sense of humour; compassionate; realistic; good communication skills; admits mistakes.

Lead from the front, or from within the ranks? Or perhaps varying positions depending on current specific situation? Quite a list, possibly leading to quite a discussion!

Share your ideas with others – is there anything you'd like to add?

Any differences between a department leader in a work situation – or a sports team, or a social group, or whatever – and a home team leader? What other qualities and skills might be valuable for a home team leader?

Any other suggestions? One useful thought from a recent discussion: don't start a sentence with *'But...'* Instead, say *'Yes, and ...'*

More practical activities – again, individual or group discussion (or both)

What are the best qualities necessary to be a valuable team member?
How easy or difficult is it to be a really good team member?
How to develop teamwork when people are based in different locations, but are all involved in support and care for one individual?
How best to build teamwork between family members and professionals?
What are the problems and pitfalls in all the above situations?
To what extent is it possible to anticipate these problems? How best to plan for these pitfalls?

Matt's story – change and consequences

After three years of good steady progress at primary school, Matt, aged nine and the youngest of three brothers, started getting into a lot of trouble at school. Several times over three months at the beginning of his fourth year he'd been called to answer to the head teacher for being rude to his teacher, interrupting class, distracting them constantly from class work by shouting out, swearing, thumping and kicking everyone around him, and kicking chairs away as people were about to sit down.

He was frequently trouble outside the classroom too, for breaking the school rules about fighting and bullying, and lack of respect for other people including school staff – a huge change in Matt's behaviour from the easy-going lad everyone had known, who had lots of friends and who especially loved football.

Matt seemed to have completely lost his sparkle and his sense of fun, he rarely smiled; his teacher reported he'd become argumentative and often rude, and the smallest frustration (which happened frequently) led to an explosion of rage.

Several times he was 'grounded' inside – after having his lunch, instead of going out to play football with the boys who had until then been his friends, Matt had to report to the head teacher's office. While he was 'grounded' he had to write essays about topics such as 'School Rules – what are they for?', 'Why do we need school rules?', 'How I like to be treated', 'What are hands/feet for?' and so on. These were then sent home to be discussed with and signed by his parents.

At the round-table discussion arranged with his class teacher Mrs M, the head teacher Mrs S and Matt's mum and dad, Mrs S explained how concerned the school staff were about the recent change in Matt's behaviour, which was affecting his school work and his relationships with the other boys as well as staff, and which seemed to have started a few months before. Matt's mum said that was around the time that Matt's dad had changed his job, driving much longer distances abroad rather than local routes, and she'd taken on some evening work to help with family finances. After more discussion Matt's parents decided to tell Matt how concerned they were, that they felt Matt was unhappy about something, and to ask him if he could tell them what was the matter.

A week later there was another round-table meeting at school. Matt's mum reported that she was going to cut her working times to two instead of four evenings a week, and Matt's dad reported that he'd decided to return to short-distance driving, and to take all the boys swimming once a week. Also, he planned to take each of his sons out with him in the lorry on a short trip at least once a month.

Within a few weeks the change in Matt's behaviour was again noticeable at school and home, but this time positive – and by the end of the school year he was once again working well within his class, in the playground and outside. He was much more like the earlier Matt everyone had known.

What happened between the two round-table meetings arranged in school? At home during whole-family discussions, Matt's parents had sat down and listened to Matt and his brothers talk about how they all felt there was little time in their parents' lives for the boys because of changed work patterns. They recognised that although all the boys had similar feelings about the huge change in family life with much less time together as a family, they had all found different ways of coping with those changes. Mum and Dad had asked what might help. Again they'd listened – and come up with suggestions to show the boys how much they cared.

But without sitting down to talk about what was happening, about how everyone felt, and about what might make a difference, nothing would have changed for Matt or his family. It's quite possible that Matt's unhappiness could have grown into even more difficult times for himself as well as everyone around him.

Repeating patterns?

Long-term family carers cope with an enormous range of health conditions: the newborn baby who shows no signs of any particular problem but is later diagnosed as having 'severe learning difficulties'; the child who, at the age of three, develops symptoms *on the autistic spectrum*; the young girl who develops mumps, and then when she returns to school gets into lots of trouble for *not listening to the teacher, not doing what she was told* until the real problem is recognised – she'd lost her hearing when she was ill. There is the young adult who heads off to university in happy anticipation to follow his dream of studying for a degree, and develops schizophrenia ... his grandma who develops Alzheimer's ... and his geography teacher who has Motor Neurone Disease. Then there are cases which defy diagnosis, such as the patient described by Oliver Sacks in his book *The Man Who Mistook His Wife for a Hat*,[8] whose perceptions somehow became scrambled and lost in total confusion.

Human experiences are infinite; I'd need another book (at least) simply to list even half – even a fraction – of the possible conditions and the infinite individual variations of each one, most of which may fit an already-recognised condition with a particular cluster of symptoms. Or they may not. Even with a diagnosis the symptoms, or any single one of them, may change as time passes – or possibly more symptoms may develop, or the same symptoms may affect people with different diagnoses and may vary in duration from fleeting to long-term effects. Again, there are no easy answers.

A person may be born with a strong healthy body and mind, may flourish and grow, enjoy good health throughout life into old age and then eventually die a peaceful death. Unfortunately, though, sometimes from birth, or at some point in childhood, adolescence, adulthood, in maturity or old age, at any time of day or night, at home or away, any part of the body or mind, nerve or tissue, muscle, bone or tendon, can be affected in an infinite number of ways. Sometimes the illness, injury or change in condition can happen very suddenly, or it may take time to develop; sometimes it can be recognised and treated, and sometimes no successful treatment is known at that time and in that place.

Years of experiment and research – plus a good deal of trial and error – have meant that more medical symptoms may be treated successfully today than in the past; change and new developments are part of life. Unfortunately this does not mean that all illnesses are now recognised or can be successfully treated. Even with well-recognised and relatively common conditions, such as arthritis where research has been ongoing for many years, new aspects may still be found.

I met two people recently who described their experiences within their own families of rare conditions, Ehlers-Danlos Syndrome and Turner Syndrome. I learned that for people with unusual or rare conditions, research and positive developments may happen at a much earlier stage, but diagnosis and finding effective treatments is much more difficult.

Character, personal choices, and even luck or fortune, may also be connected with and affect all the different experiences and situations found within even the tiny section of humanity I've met or know of. Whatever the illness or condition, individual personality and character can be, and often is, crucial to the eventual outcome.

While Annie doggedly practices her recommended exercises three times a day, increasing the number or repetitions every week until the strength is built up around her hip after a hip replacement operation, Aggie – who occupied the hospital bed next to Annie – refuses from the start to even try the exercises, and complains bitterly about the 'unfair demands' of the nurses and physiotherapists (and her visitors) who are trying to help and encourage her. No need to guess which of the two, a year later, can walk for miles without a stick and climb stairs ... and which one rarely leaves the house, struggles on stairs, and complains endlessly.

Joe takes his medicine as instructed and ensures he attends all appointments, while Michael, who has the same diagnosis, doesn't bother much about medication or appointments – despite the frequent reminders from his family and the despair they express.

Perhaps you can recognise some similarities to one or more of the situations described here. Whatever your own circumstances, experiences or situation, as in *all* these scenarios, family members can and often do make an enormous difference – can often recognise a particular behaviour pattern developing and work out how to offer the best possible support. All of this, as we have seen, depends to a great extent on good all-round communication.

Relapse: recognising individual signs?

There can be a range of different 'relapse' behaviours in just one diagnosis. For instance – Simon, diagnosed with schizophrenia, was often suspicious of people, but in the week before he began to relapse, his paranoia would grow ... and his family realised that when this happened Simon needed extra help and they would seek medical advice. This early recognition and help has meant that Simon has avoided re-hospitalisation for much longer periods of time.

On the other hand, although the same diagnosis has been given to Vi, her family recognise that when she starts to obey the commands of the voices she frequently hears – rather than ignoring them, as she usually does – this is a sign of approaching relapse. Again thanks to this early recognition, Vi too has often been able to avoid re-hospitalisation.

P, also diagnosed with schizophrenia, is usually an early riser but when he begins to relapse he feels lethargic and stays in bed until his mother insists he get up. K, on the other hand, has the opposite pattern, usually staying in bed until midday or even later but unable to sleep at night or during the day and becoming hyperactive when heading for relapse.

Finally, in James's case:

> 'Most of the time he eats with us, takes part in family activities. But when he's heading for relapse, he stops eating with us, stays in his room most of the time. We know all the signs, we've seen it so often over the last years. And sometimes we can talk to him, persuade him to take his medication again – when he's going to relapse he doesn't believe in the diagnosis, doesn't think he needs medication, and he stops taking it.'

When at last my beloved Jay turned the corner and began to fight against the twin demons rather than everyone around her, I began to recognise a pattern of progress for a while, followed by a setback and a return to alternate self-starvation followed by binge eating and getting rid of all sustenance ... followed by a more settled period when she fought anorexia and bulimia to establish better nourishment. Gradually the settled periods of self-control extended and the setbacks grew shorter and shorter until Jay was back in firm control of her diet and eating habits, and her behaviour.

Personal stress may be connected with work or school, social or home situations, and it appears to be a common factor in triggering difficult symptoms and behaviour – and also in triggering relapse. One night my daughter, by that time well on the way to recovery and again living independently, phoned me to talk about a very difficult situation at work. I could recognise the stress in her voice, and I tried to enquire calmly and quietly if her eating had been affected. '*I can hear what you're saying, Mum,*' she said, '*but don't worry. I've been there, done that – I won't be going back!*' I was extremely thankful that she had been able to recognise the signs.

Relapse management or even prevention – *how?*

Recognising the possibility of relapse is a major step towards being able to do something to avoid it, or at least to avoid the worst of the symptoms or shorten the duration of increased problems. *Coping with Schizophrenia – a Guide for Families*[9] gives a practical chapter on Early Warning Signs of Relapse, such as social withdrawal and depression, anxiety, tension and irritability, eating problems, sleeping too much or too little and decreased compliance with treatment – not unlike those signs reported by families supporting someone with an addictive/compulsive condition – and also outlines some strategies for coping, such as walking, doing puzzles, reading, or hobbies.

In the case of eating disorders, the Maudsley Hospital has carried out studies into how to avoid relapse, with changes in food habits being identified as a good indicator of relapse, as well as avoiding social contacts. From these studies, collaborative treatment which involves home carers – rather than treatment away from family – has been developed.[10]

These are studies related to only two conditions – perhaps it would be interesting and worthwhile to try to find out about such studies in condition(s) affecting your own family and situation.

How can home team members help to prevent relapse?

Finding times when your loved one is coping well can be really important so you can:

- talk about their progress, stressing the positive efforts you've noticed them making and how much you appreciate those efforts
- check what they feel has helped most to bring about that progress – and anything that really doesn't help
- find out how family members and friends can recognise the early signs of relapse
- find out how best the family can help if they recognise signs of relapse.

This is where a regular Family Forum can be really valuable – recognising a repeating individual pattern of relapse can lead to discussions of how to lessen and possibly even avoid the impact of such a relapse, and how best to offer help and support.

Over recent years, similar studies have also been carried out in other conditions. The stories quoted in this book are only a few from many millions worldwide, about how each of these families developed better support for *everyone* in the family through building their 'home team', with good communication and working together through awareness and discussion. Without that essential teamwork and discussion, little is likely to change for the better.

Co-ordination, collaboration, cooperation, consistency, constructive communication...

As we have seen, meeting together and talking about the situation and issues affecting everyone is the most important ingredient for developing effective co-ordination of the best care and all the other Cs we've already noted – perhaps through 'Family Forums' as noted earlier, or over a meal or other shared time together. Even sharing time together connected by Skype is better than no contact at all when someone in the family lives at a distance. The important thing is keeping in touch with what is happening, with any developments, with how people are feeling. For instance, if you – or the main carer – are exhausted caring for a long-term and distressing condition, coping with all the emotional as well as physical stress involved in supporting a loved one through cancer, perhaps consider asking a friend or family member to take on the job of answering the phone or other enquiries?

Situations and issues rarely remain static, so 'family forum' meetings need to be regular. When someone really can't make it to a particular meeting due to another unavoidable commitment, someone who *can* attend the get-together may volunteer – or be asked – to pass on what was discussed.

Is all communication constructive? Unfortunately, no. Discussion of disagreements and differing views can be very constructive indeed in finding a way through tough times and challenging situations – as long as everyone considers carefully what they want to say about how they view the situation and any ideas they have for working through difficulties, *and expresses their thoughts and feelings calmly.* This will involve careful consideration by everyone beforehand of the items previously agreed for discussion, and will involve everyone considering other people's feelings – which some folk find more difficult than others.

No solution?

When much time and discussion has been spent on a single issue and no solution has been agreed, it can help if the chairperson suggests coming back to that issue later – at the end of discussion of other issues, or perhaps at another time. Everyone could be asked to think about that specific issue, and if it is generally felt necessary, a separate meeting may be suggested/agreed to discuss that item calmly and consider all aspects.

Compromise?

Sometimes no real agreement can be found, and rather than risking carrying on and perhaps creating bad feeling, *compromise* or *agreeing to differ* may be a way forward. The issue can perhaps be reviewed again in the future to find out if it is still causing difficulties, and if all efforts within the family fail to resolve the issue, perhaps it might be time to seek help from someone outside the family to act as a peace-maker.

Family Teamwork? – cooperation, co-ordination, calm and consistent collaboration, constructive communi-cation... Or, in other words, everyone 'singing from the same song sheet', with harmonies and interesting individual variations.

Single home carers

Whether the patient has a mental or physical condition, whether it is common or rare, having a whole capable family around them plus friends and neighbours – or perhaps a family where every member 'fights their own corner' but still cares about other members – often seems to be easier than struggling alone as a single family carer. Even when the person at the centre can recognise the problems caused for themselves and others, for a home carer struggling alone 24 hours a day that lonely battle can seem twice as difficult. With family and caring friends around (no matter what their perceived faults and foibles!), at least there's the *possibility* of a combined and collaborative effort to offer whatever support they can. If there is one within reach, a self-help or other carer support group can be really valuable here – more about self-help and support groups later.

When I met with Ronald and his son Steven in rural northeast Scotland, Ronald told me his family story and of his life as a single family carer:

> *Like his brother, Steven was a very bright outgoing boy – until he was 8. The first sign was when he seemed to go into puberty ... the doctor thought possibly an endocrine problem and a hospital appointment was arranged ... a brain scan found a tumour which affected his pineal gland and affected growth. Various options were discussed. Anne, my wife, and I decided that rather than sending Steven hundreds of miles away to Great Ormond Street, we would 'go local'. He was in Aberdeen Sick Children's Hospital for a year with no communication, no speech.*
>
> *Then gradually his memory returned, and his speech – though slow, he could converse quite well. Now 38, in the last couple of years Steven speaks without expelling air. Steven has a ventricular shunt – a plastic tube that goes from the ventricles in the centre of his brain down into his peritoneum to drain fluid from his brain – over the last 30 years this has blocked about six times (which is potentially fatal) necessitating emergency brain surgery. When this happens it's quite frightening and very difficult to cope with; that and the recent development of testicular cancer. Steven is also quadriplegic.*
>
> *When he was well enough, we considered various options for continuing his education ... and the Warner report[11] spoke of 'care in the community' and integration; government legislation emphasised creating facilities, e.g. ramps, to allow wheelchair access. So after exploring and considering options – such as residential care in Edinburgh, which, due to the distance involved, would have made it very difficult to*

have him at home at weekends – we again decided to 'go local'. And thanks to government instructions and adaptations to the building, he returned to our small village school, Ordiquill, and later went on to a nearby secondary school.

A carer was employed to support Steven at school, and after gaining Higher Maths, Latin and French and Standard Grade English, Steven was reviewed by a lecturer with regard to going on to tertiary education ... Thanks to Steven's achievements, there has been a major change in attitudes towards pupils with physical handicaps.

Again various possibilities were explored ... locally, at that time Moray College was unable to give wheelchair access. Steven then applied for Motherwell College, some distance away, to go on to further education in computing, and was accepted – but unfortunately the college didn't have the right residential accommodation to allow someone with severe disability to take up the place; the cost of his living care was assessed and we could not meet the entire cost. When we asked for help from our local MP, he was very helpful. Around this time, Steven began having epileptic fits, and started medication to stabilise the condition.

By that time Moray College was adapted for wheelchair access – so Anne gave up her job as a Maths teacher and drove him to Elgin every day (about 40 miles from our home) to attend Moray College and study computing.

I was back at work then, as a school dentist travelling round the schools with a dental caravan – I enjoyed my job and every year in several primary schools I was asked to be Father Christmas! So I kept wellies in the boot, just in case.

Anne's life revolved around Steven – I do regret that Anne didn't have an 'outside' life then. I've realised it's really important to keep some life to yourself; it makes you better able to cope. At first we did it all ourselves ... we worried about what would happen if one of us wasn't fit. So we asked for someone from Deveron Care to come once a week to shower Steven; this was later increased to every day.

Our other son Stuart must often have felt Steven got all the attention – he was five when Steven developed the brain tumour. I do feel Stuart lost out ... music really helped, he loved music and thanks to encouragement at school he played the tuba and entered competitions. He did very well at school and went to Oxford, where he gained first class honours in Physics. He did research in astrophysics and completed his PhD in that. He's worked all over the world now, doing research and lecturing. And yes, he still likes playing music, especially classical!

Six years ago Anne developed a brain tumour, and in a very short time she died. Now – I do the vast majority of Steven's care, but it's really important to share Steven's care, for his sake as well as my own. There's respite care every Monday and Wednesday afternoons and on Friday mornings, which gives Steven a chance of experience with other people and gives both of us a chance to broaden our horizons. For a time, social life was non-existent. Then we heard of a concert we both wanted to go to, and found out about events and venues where there's wheelchair access – sometimes the 'wheelchair access' was four big guys lifting the wheelchairs upstairs – later, venues installed lifts. Then we started going all over Britain, checking every time on access for wheelchairs. We go to a show or a concert at least twice a month – we're booked up for shows etc. up until July next year, nine months ahead! Great to have something we can share, something we both look forward to.

Now the government has delegated some money to carers to help them organise for themselves what they need – I can get a carer to help Steven so we can do more trips in the car or by train, someone to help look after him.

The very best thing was taking Steven on holiday to Paris … I needed someone to help lift Steven, so a nurse agreed to come with us, plus my cousin. We took the train from Keith to Aberdeen, then on to London where we stayed in a central hotel near King's Cross station. Then the Eurostar to Paris, where we found a hotel near the Gare du Sud. There were lifts onto trains for a wheelchair. We wanted to see Paris, found out about a taxi minibus – the wheelchair was no problem at all to the driver, he had a wonderful attitude. He took us to all the well-known sites, for instance the Eiffel Tower and Montmartre. He picked us up again the next day and we went on a Seine boat trip, and then shopping in Paris – the best trip ever! My only regret – we didn't do it years ago, with Anne.

*Often the people who help are not the ones you expect –
when Steven was diagnosed, some people avoided us. It was
the same when Anne died. People we knew – some people
didn't even acknowledge the diagnoses for Steven or for Anne,
or Anne's death. You don't have to do much, just be there.*

Ronald

Throughout all the challenges and very tough times he and
his family have encountered, Ronald has explored options and
asked for the help he needed to build the most effective care
possible and create a good home team for all the challenges he
and his son have met.

In your own situation:

Try to find out as much as you can. Think carefully about
what help you need in your own situation, what you want to
say and how you'll say it, and *ask* your own home team for
help in coping with particular problems or situations. *Ask* your
family and friends if they can suggest anything you haven't
thought of … *ask anyone who you think might offer different
ideas to try.*

Ask healthcare professionals you come into contact with,
bearing in mind that as noted in Macmillan Cancer Support's
Hello, how are you?[12] booklet, healthcare professionals don't
always have all the answers – try to find out as much as
possible about each individual's role, which will help you to
turn to the right person. To help them to work out what's
needed, give them as much up-to-date information as possible
about your own tough times and those of the vulnerable person
you're caring for.

If one person can't suggest practical ideas, *ask* if they can
suggest someone else who may be able to help.

Remember *– change, even in the best of times, is rarely easy
and usually takes time and effort for everyone involved.* With
really tough times, when people are under personal stress
at home as well as coping with whatever is happening in
their lives outside their home, often communications become
fraught and tempers are frazzled, making life even more
difficult. This is especially true when feelings have become
tangled by disjointed communication, a lack of shared

information and possible disagreements on what information might mean.

Think of how many times your own family sits around the same table during a week or month, talks about family matters and listens without interruption when others express their own feelings – and how many separate conversations may take place over the same time, not to mention different possible interpretations of those separate exchanges and incidents...

Remember, not everyone can listen and respond in the same way – and there may be lots of trials and errors along the way. But without even exploring options and possibilities for positive change, who knows what could be achieved?

Notes

1 Belbin, R. M. (2004) *Management Teams – Why they Succeed or Fail.* 2nd edition, Elsevier.
2 *Chambers' Giant Paperback Thesaurus* (1995).
3 Sams, J. and Carson, D. (1988) *Medicine Cards.* Bear and Company, Sante Fe, New Mexico.
4 Greene, R. W. (2010) *The Explosive Child.* Harper.
5 *Radio Times*, UK (3–9 April 2010) – interview with Professor Martin Elliot, surgeon, Great Ormond Street Hospital.
6 Covey, S. R. (1999) *The 7 Habits of Highly Effective Families.* Simon and Schuster, UK.
7 *Proactive, Planned and Coordinated: Care Management in Scotland* www.scotland.gov.uk/publications April 2010 (Accessed on 15/5/2014).
8 Sacks, O. (1985) *The Man Who Mistook His Wife for a Hat.* Touchstone Books.
9 Mueser, K. T. and Gingerich, S. (1994) *Coping with Schizophrenia.* New Harbinger Publication, USA.
10 www.national.slam.nhs.uk/eatingdisorders (Accessed 15/5/2014).
11 Warner, N. (1992) Choosing with Care: The report of the Committee of Inquiry into the selection, development and management of staff in childrens' homes. HMSO.
12 Macmillan Cancer Support, *Hello, how are you?* www.macmillan. org.uk (Accessed 15/5/2014).

6

Communication
Constructive or not?

Communication, good or bad, can make or break a situation and change it completely. Therefore, building constructive home team communication is extremely important when every area of life can be affected. Easy peasy? NO!

Even in those relatively uneventful times when life is running reasonably smoothly – remember those? – being aware of how others feel means tuning in to those small clues of expression and tone, as well as choosing our words to suit time and topic.

Often within our own families we assume that the people around us – who share our daily lives and some of whom we may have known since birth – understand us better than others, know our deepest thoughts and hopes and fears, joys and sorrows, know our feelings about daily situations and experiences, somehow know about our love and appreciation *without us ever actually saying the words.* In turn they often assume the same of us.

While most of our days are filled with minor events that cause little or no thought or comment, passing without any special attention, a minor event can begin a major life change … perhaps just a few words, such as *Great! – thanks for remembering to bring down your washing – and you've brought all the rest down too!* In the scale of things, this is such a tiny thing really, but commenting can show that you noticed and really appreciated it. This may possibly be the beginning of many more helpful actions, each small on their own but greatly adding to the smooth running of the house.

Which areas of home life may be affected by long-term illness?

Mealtimes? Cooking? Shopping? Time? Household chores? Heating? Finance? When Jay was so ill, almost every area of home life was affected:

> Mealtimes – *to comment or not on unusual eating behaviour? Try to persuade to eat or not?*
>
> Cooking – *difficult to produce a family meal when half the ingredients are missing (although they were bought yesterday)*
>
> Shopping – *forget bulk shopping, it might encourage bingeing*
>
> Time – *more time needed for extra shopping*
>
> Heating – *low body weight means extra heating*
>
> Use of kitchen and bathroom facilities
>
> Finance, relationships, social life, sleep, work and concentration ... *not to mention feelings of frustration and worry about not knowing what best to do to help, and personal isolation.*

How is YOUR home life affected? Consider all the areas above and think how they may be affected in your own situation. Are any other areas of your home life affected?

What about your family communication – fraught and frazzled?

Few people live in complete isolation – even when living alone, even with no family members living nearby, most people have friends, neighbours, colleagues. Whatever the situation, each interaction, no matter how minor and unremarkable at the time, may be interpreted in different ways, may be of great importance to one person or more. In any day small gestures such as a smile, or a hand held out to help board a train or up steep steps, can be a turning point – and on the same day, so can a frown, or being ignored by everyone around while struggling to cope with a situation that is causing the individual difficulty.

Lack of cooperation, getting angry, fooling around, or misunderstandings because of distorted thinking? Every action can trigger a reaction and affect others in the group in a ripple effect. When 'difficult' behaviour becomes a regular feature, this will inevitably have a long-term effect on the everyday life of other people, as well as consequences for the individual. (For definitions and more discussion, see Chapter 4, *Challenging Behaviour*.)

In our ordinary everyday home lives, things often drift along, revolving around work times, social and other activities, with mealtimes to fit in with these, and everyone busy dealing with their own world. *Where are my specs?! I'll be late... Your mum called, ring her back. Is there more cereal? You forgot to...* It is all too easy to miss the small indications giving us clues about how other people feel: body language, facial expression, perhaps a change of pace, increased or perhaps a complete lack of interest.

To create the most effective ongoing all-round 24-hour care, and the most therapeutic environment where everyone involved can play a supportive role, good communication is *essential*. All those small comments and actions are now even more important for the whole home team.

Constructive and effective communication – how?

Whether at home or at work, whether in good times or tough, just a few of the qualities needed are:

- good listening skills, awareness of body language, facial expressions
- personal patience
- relevant information
- generosity of spirit – when someone is unwell they may not act or speak as they usually do
- **no** assumptions which may or may not be based on fact and accurate information, or possibly even on someone else's assumptions.

All of these may be affected by tiredness and other distractions ... and all of them may affect communication, may lead to constructive effective and supportive conversations. Without them, the opposite is much more possible, leading to difficult scenes and destructive conversations. These will inevitably undermine the possibility of effective care ... let alone 24 hour best care in tough times. Where to start?!

Pace of life (breakfast)

Growing a healthy relationship

Any relationship may be compared to a delicate growing plant: in the right conditions it will flourish and grow well. With a plant, this will involve the provision of the right amount of light, water, space and heat. Unlike humans, usually plants come with useful information and instructions, either verbal or written.

But when conditions are not good, or perhaps when they change for some reason, the plant – or relationship – may struggle and even die. The difficulty may develop quickly and have drastic effects, or it may grow over a long painful period of time. The sooner the struggle is noticed, and the sooner constructive action taken, the better ... more or less shade, more or less direct sun, more or less water, space or warmth. *But without any information or support, deciding just what is best to do or avoid doing will not be easy or straightforward.*

Like a growing plant, changing just one aspect in a relationship – or perhaps several – will also affect other aspects. Unfortunately just one destructive conversation may cancel months of positive growth, perhaps when one of the participants is under pressure, hasn't had enough rest or sleep, has distorted perceptions or makes wrong assumptions.

First it is necessary to work out what best to do.

Communication within a home team

Depending on the personalities of the people involved, within *any* group living or working together in close contact there will be differences of approach, differences of perspective, differences of opinion. This is true for any class of children from an early age – and for the staff teaching them; for a group of soldiers; for a team of athletes; a board of directors for a company; doctors, nurses and other staff in a hospital department; and for families and other home teams. *Whatever* the group, as always each person will bring a very personal mix of background, experience, beliefs, ideas, training, perceptions, understanding and so on. As always, when one member of the group changes, the whole group will be affected.

Whether living in a small wooden structure or grand mansion, a semi-detached bungalow, a city skyscraper flat or a rural farmhouse, the action within the home will be interlinked among all the members. Even in the very best of times, misunderstandings can arise and disagreements may occur.

Practical activity

Think of any group you belong to, perhaps at work or linked to an interest, activity or hobby.

Think of what happened when one of the established group left. What difference did this make to the rest of the group?

Now think of when someone new joined the group. How did that affect relationships within the group? What about communication – what effect did the new group member have, if any, on relationships and communication? Think of when one of the established group became unwell, or when someone's behaviour changed due to stress. Perhaps more distracted and forgetful, or more irritable? How did this change in behaviour affect the rest of the group?

As always, everyone sees what happens from their own perspective – and reacts from their own mix of personality, background, understanding and experience.

Emotional or mental health problems? Here is just one example of how the behaviour of one person can affect others:

Living with Obsessive Compulsive Disorder (OCD)

Simon won a scholarship to a private school – we were all so proud of him. But in his second year there, the school phoned and asked me to go and collect him; they wouldn't tell me what was wrong. I drove down there as fast as I could. He was sitting rocking incessantly on his bed, holding his head in his hands. He hadn't been to classes for days, told me he couldn't go because of the germs. Hadn't eaten for days. I could hardly recognise him. When I said I'd take him home, he got really distressed about packing all his things because, he said, everything was 'filthy'.

I thought he'd be pleased to get home to his own family, with all his own things round him. But when we got home he looked at the room he'd shared with his brother Jake and said he couldn't sleep in there, there were 'germs everywhere'. But there was nowhere else for him to sleep, so he insisted that he 'had to clean the room' even though I'd cleaned it the night before. He still does, he cleans it every day – over and over again, always at the same times, always the same order of cleaning. Just one of his rituals. And if he decides something isn't quite right when he's finished, he has to do it over again. Every day we just hope that the cleaning stuff doesn't run out – then all hell breaks loose. We found out he was self-harming too.

Jake decided to sleep in the attic so Simon could have the room to himself. Now, five years on, Jake is at uni and they don't communicate much at all. And my husband has constant rows with Simon, tries to get him to relax a bit and not focus so much on his rituals. Rows with me too, says I make excuses for Simon.

What's going to happen to Simon? To our family? I wish we could go back to before OCD invaded our lives. I wish someone would tell us how to help him, help all of us.

Mary

Like Mary, who felt her family life had been taken over by OCD, I found that it helped me to think that two unpleasant and very unwelcome characters, Anorexia and Bulimia, had taken over Jay's life and personality, while Alzheimer had taken over my mother's life. Whatever the illness or condition, this idea can help to separate feelings about the difficult behaviour and the person you knew before illness took over. In other words, 'Separate the person from the problem'.

We had great fun when we were growing up, shared the same room for years ... talked all the time. I miss her so much, the sister I knew, all the daft fun we used to have, dressing up and stuff. I do try to help her, I know it's not her fault but it's hard. I don't really understand, don't know what to say now. Mum and Dad are always fighting, sometimes Dad doesn't come home now. I'm worried they'll get a divorce. I wish we could all just sit down together and sort it all out.

J, personal contact

Practical activity

Think of any behaviour in your own home or family group which has changed. Make a note of *what* happens, *who* the behaviour affects, *where* it happens, *how* it affects you and other family members.

Reread your notes. Does the behaviour fit the definition in Chapter 4, *Challenging Behaviour*? Is there anything you'd like to add?

On a scale of 1 to 10 (*relaxed and happy* to *fraught and frazzled*), make a note of the effects of the behaviour on you, and on other individuals.

Add a note of *why* you think your family member's behaviour happens – e.g. a health condition may be identified; individual reaction to feelings of personal pressure or unhappiness; alcohol or drugs; increased frustration because of...

Now add a note about *what the consequences are*. Note down personal reactions to the behaviour and consequences in terms of the effects on relationships.

Whatever the situation, a myriad of individual factors will play a part in positive change – or not – in terms of the recognition of an individual's problems. Without that initial recognition, often in denial of the effects of their behaviour(s), any treatment and attempts to help are likely to have limited effects. With that recognition and acknowledgement comes a window of opportunity. In each situation, communication will play an important part in helping to encourage that positive change – or not.

At last treatment begins

How often can any professional see any one individual in a busy day or week or month? How much time can be given to any one appointment? An hour a day? Or once a week, once a month? Or something different?

The rest of the vulnerable individual's time will be spent at home with more informal care, hopefully with family, friends and neighbours around, and possibly – though not always – community support workers, mental health nurses and/or social workers and others. However, even in the best of times, if a highly motivated home team is not clued up with relevant information they might miss opportunities, for example to feed in appropriate support, encouragement or reminders (those small words and interactions again). See Chapter 8, *Motivating Towards Positive Change*.

***

What might help in a really tangled home situation and with all the unproductive communication that is creating it?

Despite the pace of modern life and all its distractions, try to find quiet moments with each individual family member to talk about how they feel about particular difficulties at home, and then broach a particular topic or situation when everyone is together and relaxed. Sounds good – but if only one or two are involved in each interaction, and it's not possible to get everyone together in one place, unfortunately the possibility is still there of differing interpretations, adverse reactions, distorted stories.

How to build such constructive and effective communication is one of the most important aspects of creating best care – and often one of the most difficult.

Remember the important factors in Constructive Communication?

Listening skills – *good or not? Patience and concentration – both of which can often be affected by personal exhaustion, lack of sleep, relevant and accurate information, making no assumptions, checking you've understood what the other person means, generosity of spirit ...* all of these will affect communication and may lead to constructive, effective and supportive conversations. Unfortunately they may perhaps lead to the opposite, to difficult scenes and destructive conversations. Yet again, where to start?

Set up a 'Family Forum' to try to discuss the specific situation – and hopefully find a way towards working through it in a more constructive way than outright war. This could be a very good first step. (For useful ideas on setting up a Family Forum, see Chapter 5, *Family Teamwork*.)

Family communication has broken down?

Where mutual support is badly affected or even completely lacking, it may be hard to feel detached enough to imagine trying to get everyone together, let alone engaging in any constructive discussion. Here it may be worth considering asking someone who is detached from the situation to help set up and chair the meeting. In extreme cases perhaps a professional might be willing to help lead and co-ordinate discussions, towards achieving better care for his or her client or patient.

And then? With everyone in the home team – or at least with most people – together at last, what then?

A few useful starter phrases and questions – choose the ones you feel are best in the situation. Use your own words. Listen quietly and sympathetically, nod or smile encouragingly – if possible without comment.

> Tell me what's been happening, the way it is for you. (Situations will appear from their personal perspective which may be very different from your own ... and which hopefully can be discussed later at a family gathering to explore the differences.)
>
> What aspect of xxx's illness/condition do you find most distressing?
>
> What do you think might help you cope better?
>
> What support do you have?
>
> Who/what could help you get through this very tough time?
>
> How can we all make a plan to support xxx through this?
>
> How can we all make a plan to support each other through this?
>
> What resources are needed to put the plan into action?
>
> Anyone got good ideas for finding more information? Maybe libraries, books, or a website, or something else?

REMEMBER...

KISS: Keep It Short and Simple. No complicated words, try for a level everyone can understand.

And LESS **is more.** *Listen* ... sensitively, and with full attention. *Empathise* ... try to imagine how you would feel in the same situation; acknowledge feelings and issues, even if you don't share exactly them. *Share* ... information as much as possible. *Support* ... offer whatever is realistically possible.

Remember – what may be trivial to you may be someone else's Big Deal which means they are not coping.

Be honest   If you don't know the answer, say so. If possible, suggest ways of finding out. Offer any help you can – but *only* if you can follow through on promises.

Do...   find and stress the positives wherever possible.

Do...   acknowledge the difficulties in any situation. (*You find it hard to cope with: xxxx's screaming tempers; or the financial problems which affect the household; or feeling so isolated and not seeing your friends.*)

Don't...   dismiss any concerns as trivial; they may not be important to you, but they are affecting another person and their ability to cope.

Don't...   give false reassurances, such as '*Everything will be fine, don't worry*' etc.

Remember – family and home teams can play an important part towards recovery, helping xxx to cope better – and *you* can help too.

Communication with the troubled individual

As with any communication, it is very important to identify what level of communication is appropriate. Whether you are talking to a child or adult, unless the right level of understanding and vocabulary is found, attempts at communication can lead to increased frustration. Again, in trying to understand the problems, LESS is more – Listen, Empathise, Share and Support. With explanations, try to Keep It Short and Simple.

Standing in someone else's shoes? All too often a pupil having difficulty with maths (as I did) will be met with total incomprehension of their problem – because to the adult teacher, with specialist degrees, long years of practice and experience in maths, the mathematical problems were *Simple, girl! Why can't you just apply yourself?!* She simply couldn't understand anyone having difficulty with something so completely obvious to her.

To anyone who has understanding and ability in any area, it is hard to understand why everyone else doesn't feel the same. A musician can't comprehend why others may not be able to hear a scale, let alone sing in tune, and being unable to hear the beat is unimaginable. In any area of life some people seem to be 'naturals' while others greatly struggle. In human communication the ability to understand another person's difficulties depends on being able to think outside one's own beliefs, feelings and emotions.

Language and vocabulary? Level of understanding?

Again, no assumptions. Just because someone is young (or any age, for that matter) doesn't mean that they can't or won't understand an explanation, and just because a year ago – or even more recently – someone understood your language, vocabulary and meaning, does not mean that your words will be understood now as you intend them. Try to work out, preferably in a calm moment, what level of vocabulary is understood – and try to fit your explanation of any situation or problem to that level. After any explanation, ask if there is anything they'd like to ask, anything that still puzzles them. Also, encourage them to ask later if they think of anything else.

Finding the right level when things have changed becomes even more important when trying to help someone whose challenging behaviour is a reaction to their individual understanding of the world around them – which can change due to changed circumstances.

> *It was only when a new speech specialist realised that my daughter often didn't understand what was going on and why something happened – and therefore felt threatened – and tried using Makaton communication with her, that things began to improve. So simple, but no-one else had thought of it. The change just from using very simple signs and words, instead of ordinary sentences, has been remarkable. Now my daughter can make her needs known – and does! – without screaming.*
>
> H, interview

> *We were terribly worried when the school phoned to say my daughter had run away from school. She'd been in trouble – again – for not listening, not doing what she was told. So she*

ran away. She used to be really good in school, always good reports for her behaviour as well as her work in class, especially in Language work which she loved. But ever since she had mumps and was off school for a while, her work hasn't been good – her teacher said she just doesn't pay attention in class now. She got in trouble in the playground too.

We hoped that things would be better after the summer holiday, in senior class with a new teacher; we thought the fresh start would help. But there were the same problems all over again, not listening and so on. We tried to talk to her but she just said everyone was unfair and burst into tears. Then after she ran away, we were called in, and the school also called the child psychologist in to see her. Guess what he said?! – that her hearing was very poor and she wasn't hearing what the teacher said ... so she didn't do what the teacher had said because she hadn't heard ... didn't get her work right because she hadn't heard the instructions... Her hearing had been badly affected when she was ill. Thank heavens this is something we can all help her with, with sign language, lip reading classes and so on!

E, personal contact

Major personal changes

Before her illness, Jay had efficiently run a house, worked full time, organised meals, paid bills, gone shopping and done cooking. Under the ghastly influence of Anorexia and Bulimia, as well as all the weight she lost, she also lost all sense of being able to cope with everyday life. At the age of 23 she seemed to regress to infancy/toddler stage, coming into my bed to be cuddled and comforted like a small child, something she hadn't done since she was very small. I'll never forget holding the frail, freezing-cold body as she cuddled into me.

Small actions like leaving a door open or the curtains not closed 'properly' might be interpreted in a totally unintended way, and what friends and family meant as concern, Jay often took as criticism and interference, expressing great rage – often in the form of another 'Hairy Jamaica', as she later called those out-of-control tantrums. Yet through it all she insisted on working full time.

Perhaps your loved one's health condition, whether mental, physical or a mix, has also led to a major change in behaviour which affects home life and all close relationships?

Spelling it out

It took some time to realise that long-standing family rules had to be spelled out in words of one syllable – for instance:

We have our evening meal together at the table.
Whoever does the cooking can choose what we eat.
Whoever cooks, someone else does the dishes.

And especially:

Leave the bathroom clean for the next person to use.

I realised that my everyday communications had to be carefully structured to enable Jay to actually *hear and understand*, again spelled out in short simple words – calm reminders whenever necessary. I also realised that it was extremely important to stress that the rules were for *everyone* in the household, and most of all to remind her how much I loved her whether she 'challenged' the rules or not.

It was no longer enough to simply say what I wanted to say, and to assume that she would understand the words and phrases I'd habitually used for many years. It was only gradually that she regained her confidence as she 'grew up' all over again over several years.

Is it inevitable that tough times will always mean deteriorating relationships all round? *No* – but acknowledging and talking about all the difficulties, and finding a way through by exploring how to build on already-existing positives, will never be easy.

'I'm no angel...'

We were in Malta a few years ago when my husband David had cramps in his hands and then difficulty lifting his arm, and he was diagnosed with Motor Neurone Disease; the specialist also told us we'd need all the help we could get. A fortnight later, David couldn't lift his arms to give anyone a hug, or to drink from a cup. He had terrible pain, life became a real struggle. Together we decided to keep things as ordinary as we could, do what we'd always enjoyed – travelling, concerts, opera, seeing family and friends. We made a plan for each day, e.g. a video or a TV programme or music we liked, inviting friends around, visiting. We decided never to say 'I can't cope' – we supported each other. Otherwise you'd just give up.

Everyone wanted to do whatever they could to help. Our grandchildren were amazing – David used to ask them to test his memory on all sorts of subjects, and they thought of ways to cheer him up and make him laugh. For his birthday they gave him 'daft' socks, really lurid in shocking pink and lime green. Those socks were a great talking point with hospital staff! And when David wore them, instead of staff just seeing another person in bed or in a wheelchair, the socks gave him an individuality that's often missing in any institutional care – thanks to the effect of the jokey humour of the socks, the staff talked to him as a person rather than treating him like a vegetable lying there.

It was really hard to see David losing his ability to do things for himself – his mind was clear and he'd always been such an independent person, always strong and always felt he was 'Right' about everything. It was really, really difficult for me to lift or move him, he was a big man and by then a dead weight.

He got soooo frustrated sometimes. Four years after diagnosis – not long before the end – he began to not recognise me, started swearing at me, calling me awful names. 'Cognitive incapacity', they called it, and 'inappropriate language'. He'd never done anything like that before; sometimes he was just horrible, really nasty to me. He wasn't the real David by then, the dementia took over. But occasionally he would speak in his own voice, tell me he loved me but the pain was really, really bad.

I always loved him but I didn't always like him – sometimes I went into the kitchen or out to the shed to cry or express my hurt or frustration or anger or whatever. He often swore at me, either out loud or under his breath, and sometimes when other people were there.

From diagnosis to dying – four years. During that time David took part in classes on diagnosis for medical students and donated his body for research. He died in his sleep, very peaceful at the end. I knew he was dying because his breathing changed. I lay beside him, held him, told him how much I loved him, wanted him to be happy, peaceful and relaxed, that I forgave him everything.

Everyone came to say goodbye; our grandchildren were wonderful and insisted that David wore his bright socks when he left the house, so they put them on for him. And when they went back to school, they said all their friends asked what had happened. When they spoke with their friends about how they had helped David, and even said goodbye to him when he died, their friends said that maybe they should go and see their own grandparents more often.

Most essential? Love and care, all-round support from doctors, occupational therapists, nurses, family and friends. Ask for what you need – people will give if and what they can. Attitude is really, really important; show gratitude for what you're given. Most of all, good communication.

Ruby Buchanan, interview

By finding ways to express how she felt about those very tough times at home, by looking for what she needed – and by helping and encouraging others to express their own feelings and offer help when they could – Ruby helped build good constructive communication all round, with the most effective care and support possible for David.

What might help in your own situation? A few suggestions

Taking into consideration age and understanding:

- Clearly restate the 'house rules' which apply to *everyone* in the household.
- Discuss why rules are important to *everyone* when people share a living space – even ask your home team to help write out those important agreed rules, using separate pieces of paper for each one, and tack them up in the kitchen?

Sharing the task may lead to more discussion as well as the additions to the kitchen serving as daily reminders.

- Discuss fairness, everyone playing their part.
- Explore options such as finding a supportive professional – perhaps someone with specialist knowledge of language difficulties.
- Find a support group of other carers in similar situations.

See also Chapter 10, *Carer Survival*.

No assumptions

Appearances may be very deceptive. What you think the problem is will be based on your perceptions and your experience – and you may be totally wrong. For instance, I worked with several children who had particular problems with reading and written language, and because of their difficulty they often fooled about in class – but their logic and reasoning and spoken language in discussion were unaffected. When answering questions or writing a story, instead of pencil and paper, what they found most useful was a tape recorder.

Also, I worked with D, who at age 7 could read fluently from very complicated adult books and newspapers – yet who had no understanding whatsoever of the meaning of the words he was reading aloud to me.

Throughout years of compulsory education in many countries across the world, apart from some children who for various reasons have struggled to understand instructions and descriptions, there have also been children who were wrongly assumed to have, or maybe to lack, various capabilities. There were many children who had difficulty with various aspects of formal education – who would now be recognised as dyslexic, for example, or as having ADHD. Rather than getting into constant trouble, they needed extra support to help them achieve their full potential.

Remember, *VIEW as often as possible* – those Very Important Encouraging Words are especially important in tough times.

Give a 'crap sandwich'?

When you feel it's necessary to bring up something awkward or difficult to mention – maybe because you know mentioning it could lead to an adverse reaction – it's important to stress that you still care for and love the person, it's the behaviour you don't like.

Wait for something positive, think about what you want to say and how to say it, and put the 'crap' in the middle, between two positives. For instance, *I love you very much, but I really don't like it when you shout at me like that. I still love you so much and want the very best for you.* Be prepared to repeat as necessary.

As always, actively look for positives, no matter how small. 'Sandwiches' with lots of positives mentioned for effort as well as achievement, while still acknowledging the negatives, could make up a real feast! In other words, praise the positive – and try to work out how to tackle the negative.

Straightforward language

While some conditions distort understandings that have developed over years, for children with autism or Asperger's Syndrome – or who are anywhere on the autistic spectrum, often undiagnosed – the world around them often makes little or no sense from the beginning, and they have great difficulty in 'reading' other people's expressions and actions. What can appear as naughtiness may be due to misunderstanding or misreading language, facial and other clues, such as a yawn, a frown, or a puzzled, irritated or shocked expression.

Whereas straightforward language is important in any conversation, it becomes even more essential when anyone has difficulty in understanding what most people take for granted and probably don't even notice in their daily interactions.

Interpretations

Jokes and metaphors, common phrases and sayings may be taken literally and cause problems. For instance, *Keep your hair on! It's a blue day today. You've got your grandma's eyes...*

I've changed my mind. Keep your eye on the ball! You're pulling my leg... Some people understand words only in the literal sense, finding it incomprehensible when 'figures of speech' or complicated references are used. For them, trying to work out what someone means by saying *'Has the cat got your tongue?'*, or making an interpretation about what it *might* mean, may cause intense frustration and possibly even lead to fear, anxiety and challenging behaviour.

Remember:
- Think about how your words may be interpreted.
- Simple language explaining what you mean, or what other people mean, can help to avoid many problems.

Teach cues for when and how to greet people, how to ask or reply to particular common questions or everyday polite responses:

How are you?
Would you like a cup of tea or coffee?
Excuse me, may I have a biscuit?
I'd like to go to the toilet, please.
Where is the bathroom, please?
Thank you.
I don't really understand, please can you explain?

Knowing when and how to ask for help and when to say *I don't know,* or *I don't understand,* or *I don't like it when...* are particularly important. Talk about this, when these words might be needed, and practice together. Without at least *trying* to talk about problems, it is unlikely that anything will change.

    Consider using pictures, flashcards, sign language to help explain facial expressions – e.g. *'When someone frowns, it means...'*

Note reactions – physical touch?

People have different ways of showing affection and feel comfortable with different levels of contact. For some people, physical contact of any kind causes problems. When physical contact is difficult, this can be particularly difficult to accept for parents and others who want to show affection in this way; no matter how kindly and loving the thought behind the touch, an individual may feel under threat and that things are out of their control – and the result can be intense frustration, sometimes expressed in aggression or violence.

Again, communication is an important key. Try to talk about how you – and others – feel. Explain what, for example, a hug means, ask what it means to them and why they react in the way they do. Discuss how different people may feel and how they express those feelings. As always, use your own words.

Heightened response to sound?

For some people, sounds are magnified to a great intensity which can cause them pain and distress. While most children love balloons, the sound of a balloon bursting or fireworks can be really frightening for some, as can other more everyday sounds which are usually taken for granted to the extent they often go unnoticed, e.g. vacuum cleaners, engines, aeroplanes, hammering and banging. For some people sounds which cannot even be heard by others, possibly in another room or even in a different part of the building, will be amplified to a distressing extent.

Heightened sensitivity to texture?

Certain materials can cause problems for some folk, particularly in clothing – what may be insignificant to most people may feel like sandpaper to their skin. Sensitivity to light, temperature, sound or particular foods can also cause problems, possibly varying in intensity from day to day.

For more information, see my 2007 book *Families, Carers and Professionals: Building Constructive Conversations.*[1]

In all of these situations, be aware. Observe, make allowances, look for solutions to the problems caused. For instance, if someone hates the feeling of a particular material, try to avoid buying clothes in that material; if the sound of Hoovering causes distress, is it possible to arrange for the cleaning to be done when the affected individual is out of the building? Someone doesn't like bright light – consider changing the lighting, or the curtains?

Whatever the problem, whenever possible, find the right time to acknowledge and talk about the difficulty in calm straightforward language. Talk about how it affects the individual, then explain how others around them feel and are affected. This often brings change, as well as easing communication for everyone involved.

Routine and habit

While routine and habit are part of most people's lives – a favourite chair, their place at the table – routine becomes much more important for anyone affected by certain conditions, for instance autism or Asperger's Syndrome. A clear outline or timetable of what will happen at certain times of day – such as morning routine, mealtimes, after school, bedtime – can be very helpful, as can discussion of what will happen in certain circumstances.

For instance:

When we get up, we go to the toilet. What else do we do? We have to get washed. We get dressed. We eat our breakfast. Then we...

You're getting on really well with that jigsaw / activity. Soon it'll be time for... (next activity).

And when someone can recognise numbers on a clock or watch. We'll have our snack / lunch / supper when the clock says...

Repetition and reminders

Frequently it is not enough simply to mention a problem once and hope it will then disappear. When behaviour has become habitual it will usually take time to change. Regular gentle good-humoured reminders can be an important key to avoiding frustration when someone has forgotten – again. This is usually much more effective than arguments.

Giving restricted choices

Would you like to eat a banana or perhaps a yogurt?

Would you like to drive your cars into the garage now or just before we eat?

Would you like to wear the red sweater or the blue one?

The choice is **What** or **When** to eat or put away toys, get up in the morning, get dressed, go to bed... not **If** they are going to eat, put away toys, get up, etc.

This can be particularly important in some conditions. Serious consequences can result from the actions of someone who hears and obeys voices that others can't hear; there are several conditions where behaviour seen as anti-social, or perhaps simply unusual, can cause unexpected and unforeseen problems for the individual as well as for home family carers, and of course not eating for whatever reason can have very serious consequences.

Perhaps you can recognise some of these instances, or perhaps you can think of others in your own situation.

Calm, consistency and structure

At all times? Under all circumstances, no matter where or when?! This can be extremely difficult sometimes, perhaps especially so when you are outside the home, where other people may look on and not understand what the background is, what the difficulty is, or what you are trying to do. They may make judgements and draw conclusions without any idea of what the whole situation is.

> *F, my son who's 9, went into a real strop in the supermarket. He started shouting and screaming, running round and hitting people, pulling things off the shelves. I tried to calm him down but it was no use. Then I tried to pick him up and carry him out but he's getting too big for that now. He was screaming and hitting and kicking me and everyone was staring at us. I guessed they were thinking I was an awful mother. Anyway, I couldn't control F, couldn't calm him down, all I could do was hold onto him and try to prevent him hurting anyone. I had to ask someone to call my husband.*

It was really awful. Soon he'll be too strong for me even to hold on to him.

Marie, interview

Diet?

Small things can sometimes lead to big changes, and trying a change of diet may help to find out if any particular food triggers a bad reaction. For example, it was proved that the food colouring tartrazine can sometimes trigger adverse behavioural changes as well as skin rashes and dermatitis.[2] See also Chapter 4, *Challenging Behaviour.*

Any sunshine on this long road?

Watching someone grow and develop through all sorts of difficult and unforeseen personal setbacks and helping them overcome the challenges to reach their very best potential may be frequently difficult, frustrating and exhausting, as can caring for any adult facing serious long-term difficulties – but it is also often infinitely satisfying. Meeting or hearing about others who have travelled similar paths, and have found ways through all sorts of tough times, can often give encouragement.

David had so many problems as a child – and always had extreme reactions no matter where he was or who was there! He needed lots of extra support at school from Learning Support staff, and we saw so many professionals and specialists. Everyone helped him to understand what his problems were and how to cope with them. We also had to learn how to support and help him.

Now David's 21. After school he went on to study Law at university for two years and was named Student of the Year, then he went on to study Criminology. He hopes to work in prison services or in Customs.

David now has good insight into his problems and knows what he has to do. His flatmates help him and support him, which makes a big difference. David's teenage sleepovers sometimes caused difficulty as he didn't sleep – he had medication to help at the time. Now as a student he's always busy with projects, and again he has difficulty sleeping, so he's back on medication for that. There are also problems if he drinks spirits. However, he recognises what he needs to do, and again his flatmates help him.

Sheila Black, interview

Also, some recommended reading *Blue Sky July: A True Tale of Love, Light and Impossible Odds* by Nia Wyn.[3]

***

Important observations

When they are living with someone, whatever the circumstances, home team members often notice all sorts of details not known, sometimes not even imaginable, to others who only see a different 'front' outside the house. With hindsight many family carers can look back and see that there were signs of the onset of illness, or the beginnings of relapse … but at first they often don't realise that these particular signs, and their observations, could be significant. This is yet another reason, most especially in tough times, to sit down regularly as a group to talk over observations and feelings and discuss what could help. Later discussions may be about what helped most, what didn't help, what alternatives could be more helpful and so on.

For over a year I've tried to persuade my daughter E to accept that she has an eating problem. Our GP won't talk to me, I don't think he believes me about her bingeing at home. She gets through masses of food and there are endless rows with the others in the family when there's nothing left.

Last night the police came to the door – she has been charged with shoplifting in a local supermarket. No-one in our family has ever been in trouble with the law before and family members are just stunned, horrified. Especially Granny.

When she was interviewed by the police and social workers, my daughter told them she took the goods because there is never enough to eat at home and she was hungry. Now I hate going shopping; this is just a small town and everyone knows us, they probably even know what E said about not having enough to eat at home. And trying to convince the professionals that there's plenty of food bought each week ... they just won't listen. All the things going on at home, all the things that are happening over and over – what should I do? What should I say to the police and social workers? To Granny? And to my daughter?

Doreen

Why give professionals information?

At a later stage, having been through a series of 'episodes' which have sometimes led to hospitalisation, family members can often identify the onset of such an episode at an early stage. This can be wonderful when positive and appropriate action is taken, but heart-breaking as well as most frustrating when no-one will listen:

I can see it coming. G becomes withdrawn again, he sits in his room and won't eat with us. But no-one will listen. I tried to phone the doctor, and the specialist, even the ward he was in before, but I was told that 'because of confidentiality, no-one can talk to you'. Maybe if we could pass on our observations at home, and a higher level of treatment was started, maybe it would avoid the worst of the relapse. How can I let Dr N know what's happening? What we've seen, what we know is probably going to happen? It's all happened before – what can we do to help G?! I feel so helpless! Why why why won't anyone listen?

L, interview

Patient confidentiality is obviously extremely important, and crucial to a patient's confidence in medical practitioners. But what if the safety of the patient could be at risk if those important changes noticed by their family members remain unrecognised by people who might be able to help avert the risk to the patient, or possibly even risk to others? Sadly, there have been many cases reported in newspapers and other media where family members have been ignored when trying to get crucial help for a vulnerable individual with distorted thinking.

Can anything be done in such a situation?

When I asked this question, Dr Harry Millar from Aberdeen Royal Cornhill Hospital replied: *'Tell the family to write a letter to the treating professional – if possible, addressed for the attention of the individual doctor or therapist giving treatment – telling them about the observations which are causing them concern and why they feel so worried. A letter will be read and filed with a patient's notes. Much better than trying to phone or email.'*

For more on contacting professionals and offering personal information, see Chapter 7, *Confidentiality – and professional/ family communication.*

Asking a treating professional for relevant information

You've been given an appointment, possibly following a long wait, and you feel nervous about the meeting in strange surroundings with someone you don't really know.

Preparation beforehand is really important – it's so frustrating when you remember important questions you meant to ask but which you forgot about until it was too late.

Remember – as always, professionals can give information about a health condition and its treatment, but without the patient's informed consent they cannot give personal – and therefore confidential – information about any individual.

What do you want to know?

Write down what you want to know, and take your notes with you to refer to during the meeting.

Ask a partner or friend to go with you – it can be good to be able to check afterwards what you remember and understand about everything that was discussed.

Ask for any technical terms to be explained whenever necessary, or any other information.

***

Is confrontation ever constructive?

In some circumstances, where a condition may regularly lead to difficult personal consequences, these may be long-lasting and difficult-to-resolve ... perhaps the loss of a supportive family member or friend following a row about the theft of money to fund the addictive habit, followed by denial, verbal or even physical aggression. The individual may suffer injury after an accident, or perhaps after starting a fight. Not to mention the possibility of family rows over things such as finance, the best ways of reacting to difficult behaviours, neighbours complaining about noise, or colleagues' complaints about work undone or not up to standard.

An apology?

Sometimes, these situations *may* be resolved by the use of the word **Sorry** – when it is heartfelt and leads to positive action to tackle and change the behaviour, this is the biggest word in the world.

At times, though, unforeseen consequences may be long-term and devastating.

Whatever the condition, when difficult behaviour becomes a frequent and major daily feature, inevitably all relationships will be affected. Unfortunately, as many home carers are only too aware, an inability or refusal to recognise these effects or even to acknowledge them can lead to self-destruction.

Mixed reactions, mixed messages?

Remember Ostrich who simply sticks his head in the sand rather than acknowledge a difficult situation? What about Kangaroo, who always wants to protect, Rhino who charges in and tries to change the situation by force ... and then there's tearful and timid Jellyfish...? *Unless a home team tries to co-ordinate their care and support, the individual at the centre will get very mixed messages about their behaviour – and what is acceptable or not in the home.* ***The problem will most likely grow in scale and effect.***

Tackling the behaviour

Remember: positive feedback first, e.g. *I care so much about you*, and then the 'crap' in the middle, e.g. *I don't like it, it upsets me when you...* Then repeat the positive – *I still care about you.*

Find your own words – think of *what* you want to say, *how* to say it, and then practise. *Remember – Keep It Short and Simple. Keep calm and your voice even. Repeat as necessary.*

Think of *when* you're going to say your piece. Is the best opportunity just after and in response to a difficult incident? The individual may not be thinking rationally, perhaps under the influence of drugs or alcohol. Maybe better to wait until everyone, including the troubled individual, is calm. Remember – if any individual's thinking is not clear, their responses may be muddled by intense feelings, or drink, or... They may not have thought things through properly. *Therefore, better to wait for the effects to wear off, or perhaps have words ready for each eventuality: during the behaviour causing difficulty, and later when everyone is feeling calmer.*

How often will you say your prepared words? Is once enough? Or will you repeat when everyone is calm, and again if and when a similar incident occurs? No matter how long-standing, if one person regularly ignores family rules – taking turns at washing up, leaving the bathroom clean etc. – this can lead to major rows, most especially if someone is seen to 'get away' with behaviour that anyone else would be pulled up for.

Confrontation can explode without warning, possibly developing quickly from verbal unpleasantness to shouting and physical threats and even actual violence. Where someone has a 'short fuse', or when 'challenging behaviour' is a feature due to a lack of understanding or frequent offence being taken, aggressive confrontational behaviour can unfortunately become a regular part of life, especially when someone sees such behaviour as a way of controlling others, a way of getting people to 'back down and back off'.

When you want or need to tackle the problems caused by someone who ignores home rules for the sake of *everyone* involved, being prepared for confrontation may be the only way to tackle the situation.

Reviewing your family rules

Assumptions are often made that everyone knows and recognises basic rules of acceptable behaviour at home, e.g. cleanliness, mealtimes, use of kitchen and bathroom, etc. – and most of the time, this is the case and life runs along relatively easily. However, when changed and difficult behaviour becomes part of the picture, 'most of the time' can seem like a distant memory. It is when difficult incidents become a regular feature of life that it becomes absolutely necessary to sit down and actually discuss *what* is acceptable – or not – and review your home rules, as well as reminding everyone *when* and *why* they are necessary for the safety and comfort of everybody, including the vulnerable individual.

In addition to accepted rules for house management (washing up etc.), families usually recognise basic rules which are mostly unspoken – not damaging property, no violence to others and so on. However, when challenging behaviour becomes part of the picture – whether this is part of teenage tantrums and testing the rules to the limit, or due to mental health problems or personal frustration – spelling out firmly and very clearly what is not acceptable as well as basic expectations (and reasons for them) becomes necessary.

For instance, as outlined in *Coping with Schizophrenia*:[4]

No violence to people or property

No smoking in bed

Everyone must bathe or shower regularly

No illegal drug use

No inappropriate sexual behaviour such as walking around naked.

Just one example:

My son went into one of his rages, and smashed up the bathroom. He did loads of damage, it was really scary. Later, when he was calmer I asked him why. He said he'd had a row with his brother – and if he hadn't smashed up the bathroom, he'd have smashed up his brother. So I suppose in one way we should be thankful, it could have been much much worse.
                                                                    Chris

Ignore the situation?

As noted earlier, ignoring those effects doesn't address, let alone solve, the problem. Often a troubled individual will have no idea about the effects their behaviour is having on others – although others understand very well that the behaviour is upsetting to other people and they see it as a means of controlling the situation. Sometimes ignoring the behaviour and its effects on others seems to be seen as 'giving permission' for the behaviour to continue, as well as causing much resentment when others see this as someone else 'getting away with' bad behaviour.

In a fraught home situation, when we are under pressure and often feeling mixed emotions of anger, frustration or fear about what might happen in the future, *no-one*, including the person at the centre, is happy with the situation. The longer the situation goes on, the more difficult and frazzled it becomes.

But – what can we do?

Tackling the situation may seem even scarier than trying to ignore it and coping with the consequences. The hard choice is: accept the situation and continue as before, or attempt to change it for the better by trying to confront the individual with the effects of their behaviour directly.

How?!?

First, can you identify what the real issues are?

- Is it the behaviour itself? E.g. shouting at others; stealing money or other items; using up overnight all the food bought for the family for a week; aggression, or even physical assault on people or property, due perhaps to frustration or lack of understanding; or the influence of drugs or drink?
- Or is it the way you and others feel about that behaviour? E.g. scared, unhappy, puzzled, upset, distressed? All of these?
- Perhaps it is both the behaviour *and* its effects on others?
- Why do you need to discuss this matter? Why is it really significant? What if you ignore the situation?

- How has the situation come about?
- Who contributed to creating/continuing the situation?
- What positive outcome do you hope for as a result of the confrontation?
- What relevant information is needed?
- What have you or others already done to try to resolve the situation?

Identify the questions which are appropriate in your own situation.

What happens when someone really doesn't understand?

This is the second time the police have brought him back. He must have gone out while I was in the bathroom. All of five minutes, and when I came out I couldn't find him! He's got no road sense now, could easily have been killed, or caused an accident.

Whatever he's doing, he gets so angry when I try to stop him or distract him. He's even hit me, he never did that before – we've been married for almost forty years, and now he hits me. I still love the man I married, but now he's not the man I married. It's like being in a nightmare, hoping I'll wake up. But I know I won't wake up to anything different now until … until…

It's hard to look at the photos of us in our good years. So many good years.

I just don't know how long I can go on coping.

Yes – friends help, one of my neighbours comes to sit with him while I do the shopping, at least I get a while out of the house to do that. And social services help too, someone comes to help with bathing him twice a week. And they've arranged respite care too for me, a weekend once a month so I can sleep and kind of recharge my batteries. Next one is a fortnight away, I'm counting the hours.

Donna

When someone develops Alzheimer's or any other condition where changes in the brain lead to changes in personality, memory and reasoning ability, not all the questions above

Family Forum

may be relevant. However, for home carers trying to cope with the relentless progression of Alzheimer's, identifying the appropriate questions, and through them the effects on individuals and relationships, is equally as important as for carers in other situations.

Discussion with the home team

As outlined in Chapter 5, *Family Teamwork* involving everyone in the home situation is the best, and possibly the only, constructive way through the situation, and this needs discussion with everyone involved. If at all possible, there should be discussion with the person whose behaviour is causing difficulty for others – although unfortunately Alzheimer's and other conditions involving such deterioration often rule this out.

However, in most cases, *no matter how difficult that discussion*, without finding a more constructive way to deal with the behaviour the situation will most likely remain miserable for the whole household – and possibly get even worse. None of which will help anyone, least of all your loved one.

Time and place?

Finding a special time when several people can attend a home team meeting may be complicated. In a fraught situation where no-one is happy, is it worth the effort? Remember that the alternative means a continuation of all the same patterns.

Calling that initial get-together – or your 'Family Forum' – can be a first effort towards the recognition and acknowledgement of the effects of unacceptable behaviour on everyone in the household, and it can lead to better communication all round. However, no matter how positive the discussions may prove, and even with the recognition of difficulties in common, changes for the better may take some time.

What do you really want to say?

As always, *preparation and working out what you really want to say, and how you want to say it, is extremely important.*

- Choose words and language *everyone* there can understand.
- Be prepared to outline specific examples of situations which have caused unhappiness for others in the household, and the consequences of these situations. Ask others at the get-together about their observations.
- Try to think ahead of possible reactions and how you'll respond.
- Try to avoid making accusations – concentrate on describing calmly how *you* feel in response to your loved one's behaviour.

A few suggestions (use your own *I* or *We* phrases):

I feel very concerned/unhappy, you often sound very angry about...

I want to understand how you feel. I feel very upset when you…
Can you tell me / us why you…
I'd like you to try to…
I'd like to help you, and maybe you can help too…
So you feel … I'd like to understand … can you explain…?
I'd really like it if you would try not to…
I'd like to sort this out…

Be conscious of your body language and facial expressions.

No matter what the provocation, try hard to Keep Calm – it is very easy to say these words when you are rehearsing, but not at all easy when under pressure.

NO blame, NO attack, NO judgement. Emphasise that you are trying to understand the troubled person, trying to help, trying to make things better all round. You want to help, you want to work with them to make things better for *everyone* – because everyone is worthy of respect and consideration. *How can we all work together to make things better?*

To help everyone, try to find agreement, or at least compromise.

Acknowledge all efforts towards constructive and positive progress.

Concentrate – as M Scott Peck[5] says, '*You cannot truly listen to anyone and do anything else at the same time.*'

The Main Aim – *Explain the Gap, Explore the Gap, Eliminate the Gap.*

Relapse and prevention plans – keep reviewing the situation

A recognisable pattern will often be noticed when all sorts of good intentions and previously-agreed changes in behaviour fade. As always, there are no simple 'one-size-fits-all' answers. Each situation is as individual as the person at the centre – even when the same diagnosis has been made for two people, or twenty, or two hundred, there will be individual differences in their behaviour, needs and treatment, situation and circumstances.

With the recognition of the invaluable support good home teamwork can give, some recent books offer suggestions to help co-ordinate relapse prevention efforts – Kim Mueser and Susan Gingerich's *Coping with Schizophrenia* has been mentioned earlier, and Dennis C Daley's *Kicking Addictive Habits Once and For All: A Relapse Prevention Guide*[6] offers a whole book on the topic! Libraries and bookshops, family and friends, treating professionals, a charity or members of a self-help group may be able to offer useful suggestions and possible useful reading or contacts in your own situation. As always, remember to cross-check any information for accuracy.

With a home team in regular contact, it's much easier to be aware of any change in routine, and also of situations that might lead to added stress for a member of that team – perhaps a change of job, redundancy, illness, reduced income or money problems, a change of routine, the death of someone close, arguments and conflicts, a change in an important relationship, increased responsibilities. Any of these may cause any individual varying degrees of worry and anxiety.

Early warning signs?

Making an *Early Warning Signs Plan* can be a very important first step in checking if anyone else has noticed the same behaviour and talking about any warning signs or negative patterns which have been noticed in past relapses. Then discuss and decide what are the best next steps. Talking over family members' observations which have been causing concern with the vulnerable individual while he or she is still well may be a good start.

Just one example – T, who was diagnosed with autism, insisted that all family members sat in the same places at mealtimes; and if anything at all changed – someone sat in another chair, different plates or cutlery were used or the table was not laid to her satisfaction – T had a spectacular tantrum. For quite some time the family tried hard to avoid such tantrums. Then, after some discussion as a family, they decided that for the benefit of everyone things had to change. Together they came up with a plan. Apart from anything else, T would inevitably meet other changes and challenges in her future life

– and they felt it was very important for T's future that she learned to accept some changes.

From then on at each meal everyone sat in a different place at the table. The result? For days, T's tantrums were indeed spectacular. All the family ignored the screaming and shouting and banging. Gradually her tantrums became shorter, faded and eventually disappeared altogether as T accepted changed patterns at mealtimes – and also realised that the changes to routine didn't mean that her world completely fell apart. The family enjoyed sharing their meals again.

Scrambled official communications

In general this is beyond the scope of this book, but for just one example, see Chapter 9, *Information and Resources*.

Again, *don't give up!* This is easy to say and very hard to follow through when you are exhausted by the sheer grind of daily efforts which are often repeated frequently without seeing any positive change, despite much effort over a long time. However, without the support and efforts of people who love and care enough to stay around in the toughest of tough times, who knows what would happen to our loved ones?

Letters

Spoken words, telephone calls, emails ... most communication is the common-place chat, observations or requests which oil the wheels of life. However, receiving a handwritten card or letter is often very special, most especially one where someone has taken time and effort to write their thoughts about incidents and surroundings. (I still keep an old folder containing some letters written to me many years ago by family and friends; their handwriting and signatures as well as their words are reminders of incidents happy, funny or sad, of people and past times.)

Maybe things are going well, or you notice your loved one is making efforts to make constructive changes, making real progress? A letter or a card can serve as a lasting reminder to your loved one of how much you love them, as well as providing a boost to them to help them to continue their efforts.

Also when things are *not* good, writing down your thoughts and feelings can be even more important. Instead of keeping a journal, some people like to imagine a person (either based on a real person or made up) and then write to them with all the feelings about their life situation.

When writing, some personal observations may be important and could be passed on – and some may be best not shared (see below).

You decide that a letter might be the best way of outlining your personal view on a difficult situation?

In informal communication, *most especially if feelings and communication have been fraught or difficult,* it is very important to take the necessary time to make sure that what you say does not risk making a difficult situation even worse. This is true in conversation, in email or talking by phone – and even more so when communication is written down, when it may be kept and possibly quoted; it is important to write what you feel clearly and calmly. Therefore take your time and reread what you've written.

Does your letter say what you really mean? Have you chosen the right words, the right tone? Is there anything you want to add, or change? What will be the reaction to your words? Is this the reaction you want? If not, what needs to be changed?

Remember – once the letter (or email) has been sent, it's gone. *Make sure your letter says what you really want to say to the recipient, and consider any possible unexpected or unwanted interpretations or reactions to your words.*

How do you think your letter will be received? Will there be any unwanted consequences of expressing your personal feelings in writing? Could these be sorted out through discussion: would you welcome the opportunity to talk the issue through? Perhaps keep the letter for a day or two and then re-read it to check it does indeed say what you feel is really important for them to know.

Creating the right impression when contacting professionals

In a hurry or in informal situations you may not have 'proper' paper at hand. However, to be taken seriously when offering important information in writing, it is worth trying to imagine how those receiving your letter might react – this is far too important to risk a dismissive reaction to a scribbled note.

For more suggestions on writing a formal letter see Chapter 7, *Confidentiality – and professional/family communication*.

Notes

1 Smith, G. (2007) *Families, Carers and Professionals: Building Constructive Conversations*. John Wiley and Sons, UK.
2 www.food.gov.uk (Accessed 15/5/2014).
3 Wyn, N. (2007) *Blue Sky July: A True Tale of Love, Light and Impossible Odds*. Seren.
4 Mueser, K. T. and Gingerich, S. (1994) *Coping with Schizophrenia*. New Harbinger Publication, USA.
5 Peck, S. P. (1990) *The Road Less Travelled*. Arrow Books.
6 Daley, D. C. (1998) *Kicking Addictive Habits Once and For All: A Relapse Prevention Guide*. Wiley.

7

Confidentiality
And professional/family communication

Definitions and consequences

Confidentiality is a very common theme mentioned by treating professionals as a major barrier to talking to family carers – and also by family members trying to find relevant information about what their loved one needs and how best to offer that much-needed support.

> Fear about breaching patient confidentiality has frequently created a barrier to effective involvement of carers in mental health care.
>
> Dept of Health, 2006 (UK)[1]

An only child living with his parents (who were also only children) who worked in a boarding school, Peter – though academically very bright – never learned the basic tasks for independent living, e.g. cooking and laundry skills. When his parents died he felt completely alone and descended into depression. That's when he met M, his main 'informal support and contact' outside medical care, who helped him explore the world beyond his front door.

During winter one year, when Peter didn't respond to phone calls M contacted the police, who reported back that Peter was very neglected and in a poor state of health. Social services agreed to support him but within a few weeks the same situation occurred again. This time, however, Peter's health had diminished to the extent that he was admitted to ITU where, within a matter of a few weeks, he died alone. M visited Peter several times in hospital during those weeks

– his only visitor – and was informed of his death by the police. M's concerns were only acted on by the police; the medical fraternity were 'too wrapped up with confidentiality'. His unnecessary death was felt by all who had supported him in his activities in the community.

Peter's story, told by M

Sadly in Peter's case, the medical definition of 'confidentiality' meant contact only with *named* close relatives – and with no way of contacting his only known relative, Peter died without the comfort of anyone he knew, let alone a good friend, beside him.

Transition stages in care

Home carers have frequently encountered particular difficulties caused by the often-dramatic change in approach when a young person legally becomes an adult and they move from 'Child and Adolescent' to 'Adult' services. In childhood and adolescence some information may have been given to parents or legal guardians about the health problems of a child, the treatments available, the best approaches to provide support at home and so on. In adult services, no matter the level of understanding or personal responsibility (which may be sometimes very restricted), the only information given – if any – is almost always to the patient.

Recently in Western medicine there has been a growing recognition that treating someone in isolation without any regard to their life outside treatment could be denying patients and clients much-needed support. Slowly – very slowly in some areas – things have begun to change, with professionals now making reference to the need for sharing relevant information with home carers. Some even offer practical suggestions about how to talk over difficult topics, e.g. Ray Owen's *Facing the Storm*.[2]

As Emma Baldock notes regarding the ethical and legal aspects of care: *'Involving carers in the treatment ... is of important mutual benefit for the patient and their family. This is because the Western culture of individual autonomy and individual rights is a potential stumbling-block to carer involvement.'* Although written in a book for clinicians,[3] the information in Emma Baldock's chapter *'An ethico-legal account of working with carers...'* can be applied much more widely, and could quite possibly form the beginning of home carers finding the much-needed relevant information they need about the local implementation of recent laws.

How does this apply in practice? Recent legislation has shown the major change in professional approaches. From the Mental Health (Care and Treatment) Act, Scotland, 2003:[4]

> The patient is the most important person in this process.
>
> Those who provide care to service users on an informal basis should receive respect for their role and experience, receive appropriate information and advice, and have their views and needs taken into account.
>
> The patient might, however, state that he or she does not wish a carer or relative to be interviewed. In such cases, the MHO should weigh up the advantages and disadvantages of over-riding these wishes.

Again, the same is true with all health conditions – although many carers, coping in a very wide range of situations, have commented that this is very different from their own experiences. How useful it would be to know of and be able to quote sections in, for example, the Mental Health Act 2003, and also the Adults with Incapacity Act, 2000, DWP[5] – or the relevant acts of government where they themselves live, and relating to their own situation.

How do these notes, quotes and references compare with the rights and responsibilities of carers – professional and family – in your own area?

Trying to find a balance between the rights and needs of patients and families, and the responsibilities of both family and professional carers to provide best care, has proved a very thorny issue over many years. *'Doctors have concerns about confidentiality – that's why they hesitate to give families information'* (Dr H Millar, Aberdeen Cornhill Hospital).

Why? As Jennifer Worth notes in her enlightening book *In the Midst of Life*, about nursing and medical services in the last fifty years, in many cases the answer is fear: *'Fear of litigation haunts the medical world from top to bottom.'*[6]

However, as Dr Millar continued during our conversation on definitions and applications of patient confidentiality: 'Doctors cannot give individual information about your loved one who, as an adult patient, has rights about their own personal information being kept confidential. But there is no reason why doctors cannot offer general information about a particular condition or illness.'

More consequences

Now I'm really worried – worried that he'll hurt someone. Or maybe himself. Last time this happened I tried to phone his consultant. His secretary said Dr F couldn't talk to me because of patient confidentiality. But I think if they'd help him now, maybe it wouldn't be so bad in the long run – last time he was in hospital for months. And he was sometimes very aggressive, even violent. How can I get them to listen to me?! Help my son now instead of waiting until it's too late?

P

P's son has been diagnosed with schizophrenia, as has Jan's:

How do I know what to do when no-one will tell me?! I've never seen anything like this before. I'm out of my mind with worry, and I just don't know what to do to help my son. Why won't anyone tell me?

Jan

V's daughter has anorexia:

It's like a revolving door, home for a while then gradually all the good intentions fade. Then relapse, long waiting lists and hospital again – years and years my daughter has been ill. When she comes home, there's no follow-up to assess how she's doing. I've never had any guidance from staff as to how I could help, they say it's because of confidentiality; it breaks my heart every time.

V

It's very difficult when I hear friends talking about their children going off and getting on with life. All our children are in their twenties. The others are all working, some have gone off travelling, some have gone to university and college, some are married and having babies. My daughter doesn't go out, doesn't bother any more about her friends. She can be very aggressive and unpleasant, yells and screams when anyone tries to talk to her about why she's behaving like this – she seems like a completely different person. And no-one will tell me what to do to help – why?! They won't even talk to me when I try to phone.

Laura

And from a patient – a comment on what recent changes in the interpretation of what 'confidentiality' meant to her. Siobhan is being treated for a drug addiction:

Now my mum comes early to pick me up – it really helps now she knows how difficult it is for me to stay on track, it makes things much better at home. The therapist said it might help if I had support at home, asked who I could talk to. So I told Mum the truth. And I can talk much easier to my mum now too.

Siobhan

When offering support for someone who is trying really hard to beat an addiction, or any other condition, it can really help for a family member to find a good relaxed moment to ask gently, *'I can see you're trying really hard. We all want to help you – perhaps it might help you if someone came with you to support you at your meetings? Or maybe collect you after an appointment? Is there anyone you'd like to help you in this way? Let me know if there's anything we can do to help.'* Then leave the choice and decision to the individual – no pressure, the offer is to help and support their own efforts in any way possible.

However, despite growing recognition that to provide the most effective care possible families **need** to have the relevant information and resources, there are still some areas where concerns about confidentiality, its definition, interpretation and application, seem to outweigh the benefits for patients of co-ordinated support.

First steps

Recognising various individual strengths and weaknesses, accepting all the help possible from all directions and somehow knitting it into co-ordinated care as well as finding all the information and resources needed – all while respecting individual confidentiality ... as we have seen, that in itself is a huge challenge. Yet it is well worth the effort to try to build the good home teamwork needed, which is so important to the individual at the centre.

Whether it is ensuring medication is taken at the right times, or helping to distract from compulsive/addictive thoughts when someone is tempted to slide back into self-destructive behaviour, recognising signs of possible relapse or simply being there to quietly support through haunting and recurring issues – rarely does that much-needed support simply fall into place. While it is critical to respect individual rights to personal confidentiality, the better the teamwork, the better the all-round care.

'What do I do when I recognise the changes we've seen before which lead to relapse?'

As outlined in Chapter 6, *Communication*, rather than trying to phone or email, it is better to write a letter giving information about your observations and concerns to the treating professional. A letter will be kept with the patient's file and may be really helpful in giving the treating professionals an insight into an individual's signs of relapse.

Writing a 'formal' letter

There are various accepted ways of laying out a formal letter, but generally just make sure your contact address and the date are at the top, everything you write is clear, and include your signature at the bottom.

- Say *why* you are writing the letter, *what* your concerns are, and *how* you think the person you are concerned about may be in need of help.

As always, think carefully about what you really want to say and how you want to say it.

A few useful phrases – use your own words

Dear Dr ...,

I have noticed a change in my daughter/son/father/mother/ friend ......'s behaviour recently, and I feel very concerned as this behaviour was one of the first signs when ...... was very ill before.

I noticed that ...

I am very concerned because ...

I feel it is important that you know that ...

At our recent meeting I felt that ...

I think a meeting with you to discuss ..... would be very helpful.

I look forward to hearing from you. (OR – I do not expect an answer.)

Yours sincerely,

- Make it clear if you expect a response – or if you simply feel that the concern expressed and information you give is important, and you trust the recipient of your letter to use it wisely.
- After you have written the letter, to ensure delivery as soon as possible check that you have used the right address and postcode as well as the right postage.

Consideration should be given to how your loved one will feel when they find out that you have given such information to their treating professional – how do you think he or she will react? If you think they will react badly, *when and how* will you tell them? What will you say?

If at all possible, share this dilemma with close members of your family or 'home team'. What are the issues involved? How important is it to share your concerns with the professionals, and why? What are the benefits for your loved one? And what consequences could there be if your concerns are not shared with an involved professional?

Writing a formal letter – important questions and confidentiality

- If you feel hesitant or nervous about writing a more formal letter, perhaps you could ask someone to help you make sure you say what you really feel is important in the best way possible. Remember that by enlisting someone's help you will be sharing possibly sensitive information, and the confidentiality of your vulnerable family member must be taken into consideration. Do you have someone you can discuss this with?
- *What is the highest priority?* Is it that the treating professional needs to know the important information you want to give? Or avoiding a difficult reaction when your loved one finds out you've shared your observations?
- No matter how important you feel it is to ensure that important information is passed on to people who could help, no matter how worried you yourself feel, how will your loved one feel – the person you most want to help? Should you tell them what you have done, and why you felt it was important?
- Only you, and your family, can decide what's best in the long term. At least being honest with the person at the centre about sharing the important information, and why, avoids the possibility of your actions coming to light unexpectedly at a later date.
- When talking to the vulnerable individual about what you felt it was important to share with their treatment providers and *why* you felt it was so important, try to choose a relatively quiet and relaxed time.
- Think carefully about what you say and choose your words to explain your concerns. As always, stress your caring and concern and your wish to help them through their long-term difficulties.

A professional breaking patient confidentiality?

Sometimes a medical professional sees the real benefit of home support for a patient, and knowing that their friends and loved ones want to help, tries to suggest to the vulnerable individual that home support could be really beneficial. However, possibly due to distorted thinking or a lack of understanding, or perhaps affected by paranoia, unhappy memories and life events, when the individual is asked who they could talk to at home, they very emphatically answer 'No-one!' In these circumstances professionals, recognising that efforts will most likely be very fragmented without cooperation and co-ordinated care, may feel unsure about how to proceed.

What to do?

Comments from several doctors and therapists:

- Continue trying to involve home carers, who spend all the hours outside treatment with the patient – but by doing so go against the express wishes of that individual (whose thinking may or may not be rational)? And risk losing the trust of my patient? No!
- Assume that the patient has valid reasons to refuse extra support and accept the situation and exclude all home carers?
- Maybe leave the subject for a while and then come back to it at a later date when hopefully their thinking has changed?

Most people have at least one person they always feel has their best interests at heart, whom they would trust to help them. It might be their mum or dad or another family member, their partner or a close friend. However, without at least *asking* about a special someone who might provide extra care and support, potential benefits for any individual patient will not even be explored. Therefore professionals can:

> *Gently ask* the vulnerable person if there is one special person they'd like to ask to share tough times with them, one special person who may be given information about what helps most, or perhaps what really doesn't help at all, which may be relayed to others in the close family. A special person who may be offered the names of useful websites or books, or the name of a self-help group. *Stress* that, if they wish, the patient can be there when this information is shared with that person.

Some people may feel slighted and hurt that their loved one didn't name them – but at this time the person in the centre, and their needs, are of prime importance. It is essential to stress that *everyone* has an important part to play, and that the more co-ordination and continuity it is possible to build, the more effective the care all round – and there will be lots of times in the future for other people to show their personal support and commitment.

Remember

Finding a calm moment and the right words is crucial. **Not** *'Do you want someone to support you?'* but *'WHO would you like to support you?'*

In their fears of possibly breaking patient confidentiality, many health professionals have indeed *erred on the side of caution*. Due to these fears, unfortunately much information about background, home situations and circumstances – which would often be helpful and relevant to understanding a patient's difficulties – has been missed. In some instances, ignoring family voices that are trying to offer information about a loved one's paranoia and aggression has led to tragedy.

As my main home carer roles were supporting Jay and my mother, my own main experience has been with eating disorders and dementia; I've quoted from that experience as well as from those of many others affected by other serious conditions. *Whatever* the condition, confidentiality is often mentioned as the most frequent reason for a lack of relevant practical information.

Preparation

*Be prepared to ask questions about the situation in **your area**.* Whatever the condition, being able to quote from e.g. National Institute for Clinical Excellence (NICE) UK[7] guidelines, which give lots of information about a wide range of conditions as well as about legal and ethical aspects of confidentiality, can be a really valuable way of preparing for discussions and asking relevant questions. However, no matter how interested you are, you may find it daunting not only to find relevant information about how to support your loved one, but also to ask questions. I certainly did!

How? I found it really important to think about the following questions. **What** do I want to find out? Which words should I use? **When** and **Where**? Will you ask your questions by letter, or perhaps at a meeting or workshop? Preparing in this way helped me to ask calmly and politely – this is very important in being taken seriously, avoiding the possibility of being dismissed.

Getting involved

With more recognition of the value to patients of informed support from home carers, who have personal experience and information which the treating professionals lack, these 'informal' carers are now being invited to join planning groups, and to help write practical course materials with the aim of developing more cooperative all-round care. Although my experience has been in Scotland, similar initiatives have been helping to develop and build collaborative care in different areas and countries.

An example: a few years ago I agreed to be part of the 'Scottish Mental Health and Well-Being Support Group', mainly made up of psychiatrists, doctors and other medical staff with a few family carers and service users representing personal experience in a range of illnesses. We visited treatment centres to review treatment and resources, including arrangements for ensuring appropriate information was made available to enable families to offer relevant support. I was then invited to join the group on whole-day visits to review various established National Health Service mental health facilities and their work. This was a major learning experience for me!

It quickly became apparent that in many treatment centres, very little consideration had been given to implementing the recent mental health recommendations about building collaborative care. Indeed, in many instances little was known about home carers or what they might be able to offer in helping build all-round care – let alone information about the difficulties for any team, home or otherwise, of 'working in the dark'. Apart from their identified symptoms and medical diagnosis, often very little is known about the life of the person at the centre.

Asking my question

After listening hard, and after much thought, on the third visit I took part in I worked out what I wanted to ask. At the end of the day, after all the group visits to wards and other hospital areas, everyone involved in the review met for a final discussion – group members, heads of various wards and departments, and officials from the government's Health Department admin staff. Very near the end of the proceedings, I gathered all my courage and finally asked my question:

> *'Starting in early childhood, I've had several orthopaedic operations on my leg and back. It's quite disorientating to go from being in a therapeutic environment – with much support, medication supervised, temperature taken at set times, established daily routines for visiting times, all meals provided at certain times, everything organised – to real life at home, where people go out to work or school or meetings or social occasions or to do shopping...*
>
> *'Being discharged from a mental health ward I'd guess must feel even more disorientating when re-entering real life. Therefore it is even more important that families know what's needed to support recovery. What information do you give home carers to ensure the best support for your patients on discharge?'*
>
> *I waited expectantly. Silence grew as everyone waited for the very reluctant answer from the highest-rank hospital professional.*
>
> *At last he cleared his throat and answered.*
>
> *'None.'*

Perhaps the discussions that day about interpretations of confidentiality and their consequences, plus the questions, helped lead to positive change.

At a later date, along with several other family members who all had personal experience, I was invited to join an Open University 'Service Users and Carers Development Group', helping the Health and Social Care Department plan and develop Honours degree courses for social workers and nurses. Similar groups have been initiated in other parts of the UK over recent years – perhaps you could share your own experience of home caring as part of a similar group in your own area, and make a valuable contribution to the development of more practical cooperative care in future?

Asking questions – and positive change

As noted, *asking relevant questions is very important* to ensure you have the necessary information about what is best to do, what to try not to do, and when to call for help. As also outlined above, it is important in raising issues which affect so many other family carers. Only if issues are raised can they – hopefully! – be addressed and positive change can begin.

Thanks to the people who have raised concerns about various treatments in the past, new legislation is now being developed. Whole book chapters – even whole books – are being devoted to how to build the best possible collaborative care, sometimes written by groups of writers with very different backgrounds and experience – collaborations which would have been unthinkable until very recently.

In your own situation

Services vary in different places, as do the offering of useful local contacts and services. ***Ask how*** NICE guidelines and the health laws regarding confidentiality and collaborative care are applied in your own area – as well as about the provision of home support for patients. ***Ask how*** home carers are given the information they need to support their care giving. By calmly asking informed questions, you may be directed to what you need – or, where support is lacking, your questions may actually lead to a realisation of the need for positive change.

Notes

1 Department of Health UK Briefing Paper (2006) *Sharing mental health information with carers: pointers to good practice for service providers.*
2 Owen, R. (2011) *Facing the Storm.* Routledge.
3 Treasure, J., Schmidt, U. and Macdonald, P. (2010) *The Clinician's Guide to Collaborative Caring in Eating Disorders: the new Maudsley method.* Routledge.
4 Mental Health (Care and Treatment) (Scotland) Act 2003.

5   www.legislation.gov.uk www.mwcscot.org.uk/adults-with-incapacity-act (Accessed on 15/5/2014).
6   Worth, J. (2010) *In the Midst of Life*. Weidenfeld and Nicolson.
7   National Institute for Clinical Excellence, UK (NICE) www.nice.org.uk (Accessed 15/5/2014).

8

Motivating towards positive change
How?

In this chapter I outline what I've learned over the years about motivation and how it affects individuals, from work experience, from a wide variety of books, from my experience as a home carer, and from so many others.

Individual motivation

Personal awareness and understanding are very important factors, adversely affected in conditions such as Alzheimer's disease. As well as personal understanding and awareness, motivation is crucial to individual action towards positive change. The first step for concerned family and friends is to work out what might – just might! – make the difference. At the same time, for the individual (who may or may not understand, e.g. in dementia; may or may not be ready to change their behaviour, e.g. in addiction) the question could be *'What will my reward be for changing?'*

As with everything else concerning human beings, motivation towards positive change will also be individual. Whether you are trying to change unpleasant and aggressive responses to what most people would consider trivia, or to gain a feeling of power and control, or to manage smoking habits, unhealthy diet, excessive gambling or drugs or drinking, *identifying what will motivate someone towards positive change is crucial to any hope of success.*

Having observed carefully to find individual triggers for difficult and challenging behaviour which affects home life and quite possibly the wider community, finding what motivates an individual to consider changing their behaviour is the next step.

Each situation will vary – what will motivate Abigail may not be relevant to Bryan, and Chris may well need a different approach again. Then there's David, Ed, Felicity, Grace, Helga...

Positive change – the rewards?

Depending on the individual, an understanding of the negative effects of their behaviour may or may not be possible, but *for any person to feel motivated towards change they have to understand and accept that their behaviour is causing problems for themselves and/or others, and they need to change – also, if they do change, that there will be benefits for them.* For instance, these benefits may include increased loving attention, better health, reduced negative effects on future health, smoother interactions with others, or avoiding or reducing particularly trying experiences (for instance, when flashing lights or certain sounds create physical or emotional pain).

'And if I don't change?'

In some situations the perceived benefits of continuing the situation may appear to the individual to be greater than those of change – for instance, the initial 'high' or perhaps an individual feeling of calm or pleasure felt with drugs, alcohol, smoking or disordered eating, with the individual dismissing expressions of concern from friends or family about other effects which adversely affect health and relationships.

Whatever the initial cause of the behaviour, perceptions can be very distorted by the substance or behaviour – and a huge amount of will-power and self-control are needed to change.

With a few individuals, behaviour which is unacceptable and difficult for other people – and which may sometimes have violent or tragic consequences – even seems to be 'hard-wired' into the brain. As with every other personality trait, lack of insight or understanding of others' reactions varies and may change from day to day, even hour to hour. It may or may not be possible for the individual to understand how other people feel. Watching a reaction of fear or pain, physical or emotional, even seems to give some people pleasure – any reaction rather than none.

In *most* conditions affecting health, for *most* people, the aim is recovery in as short a time as possible. Information is sought as well as expert care and advice, appropriate assessments are carried out and advice followed. The affected individual is keen to do whatever is necessary to aid their own recovery, whether this involves an operation, taking medication, taking steps towards weight change, taking more exercise or perhaps changing certain activities. For *most* people, the motivation to be as fit and healthy as possible is already there, so that life can be lived to the full without restriction.

Distorted perceptions?

In some conditions, clear personal perception is distorted by a lack of understanding. Here again, motivation to change to more acceptable behaviour can be encouraged by noticing and praising the positive, while working to tackle and change the negative. Pay attention to and reward acceptable behaviour with warmth, praise and encouragement, and show displeasure at unacceptable behaviour with a frown, a shake of the head, and then completely ignoring the behaviour. In other words – *no reward, no attention* for the unacceptable actions or words.

In addictive and compulsive conditions – and sometimes more than one of these conditions can affect the same person – individual motivation to change is often lacking. Self-esteem, thinking and perception are often skewed by their condition, their compulsions and addictions – with a common reaction being complete denial. *'It's not my fault, it's always someone else's fault!'* is frequently part of the problem. This can be complicated even further by responses that vary greatly depending on the individual's mood and also on fluctuations in their compulsions and addictions.

One person may decide to change the negative behaviour when they finally recognise that they are liable to lose a much valued relationship. For others, this motivation may be the threat of losing their job, serious health problems, the loss of friends and contacts, or personal isolation. Sometimes it can be a devastating mix of several or all of these.

One of the best illustrations of motivation is told in the old folk tale of the Sun and the Wind in their battle to get a man to take off his coat.

I'm much stronger than you are! boasted the Wind to the Sun.

Oh really? replied the Sun. *Prove it.*

No problem, said the Wind. *See that man just coming out of his house? He's wearing a new coat.*

The Sun waited to see what would happen. *He looks very smart.*

I'm going to make him take it off! And the Wind began to blow up a storm.

The Wind blew and raged and battled with the man. But not only did he keep his coat on, the man did up all the buttons. *Brrrrrrrr!* The Wind was screaming at him, buffeting him, pummelling every part of him. The man turned up his collar and held on tightly.

At last the Wind was completely exhausted and gave up.

Then the Sun smiled on the man – and he turned down his collar. The Sun shone gently, warmly, on the man. The man undid all his coat buttons. The Sun kept on gently surrounding the man with warmth, encouragement, caring and kindness ... and the man realised that he needed to change. At last he took off his coat.

***

First steps towards change

There are several steps towards change to be made by any individual, with the first step being to *recognise and acknowledge* that there is a problem and it is having a negative effect on the individual's life.

Alcohol, for instance. With even a relatively small amount of alcohol, negative effects may involve physical problems such as poor sight and responses, or a lack of co-ordination often leading to an increase in accidents. There can be mental and emotional effects too: distorted perceptions, lack of judgement, an increase in arguments and sometimes violence, a decrease in understanding or even caring about possible consequences. With regular increased intake of alcohol or drugs, or gambling or unhealthy eating patterns, especially over a long period of time, the negative effects will also inevitably increase.

When *anorexia* takes hold, the negative effects of self-starvation appear along with a very distorted perception of body image.

Whatever the cause – sometimes even a devastating mix of several compulsive behaviours – the distorted thinking will inevitably lead to serious physical as well as mental and emotional consequences. As in all conditions, the earlier the recognition of these negative effects, the better the chance of recovery and the less likelihood of the condition becoming chronic.

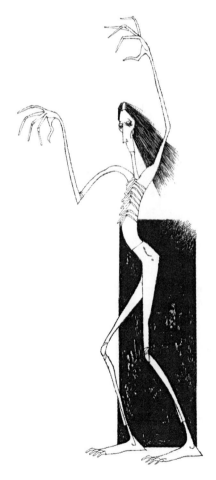

A creature called Anorexia

Are there recognisable stages in developing any addiction or compulsive behaviour? And for home carers too?

Not only are there recognisable common patterns, the term 'co-dependent' has been coined to describe the common reactions of many carers who are trying to make sense of life alongside someone affected by any addictive compulsive behaviour.

In his book *Recovering Together – how to help an alcoholic without hurting yourself*, Arthur Wassner[1] outlines that common pattern and some common reactions. Not everyone will follow the pattern in exactly the same way, but there certainly seem to be strong similarities – perhaps you can recognise the sequence from your own or a friend or loved one's experience?

Some of the steps on that slippery slope

Wassner describes how the 'Compulsive Addictive Behaviour (CAB)' commonly affects and changes the lives of individuals who react to changes produced by his/her use of substance or behaviour – and notes how main carers or 'co-dependents' frequently react to those changes. Then, as the use of the substance or the behaviour becomes more regular, the individuals may seem exciting and romantic, even 'glittering'. Social life begins to include that substance and behaviour … and often the main carer goes along with those changes and tries to fit in.

As the substance becomes a growing preoccupation for one partner, the main carer begins to accept that preoccupation, and as tolerance of the substance or behaviour increases, the main carer tries to accept or ignore – or even defend – the increased behaviour while trying also to ignore their own fears.

Sooner or later, the main carer becomes frustrated with lapses caused by the substance or negative behaviour – while sometimes also wondering if it is he or she who is crazy.

Then comes guilt about the use of the substance or behaviour, with CAB making efforts to hide it. The main carer feels appeased by that guilt and accepts the promises of change.

Unfortunately in this common downward spiral, most often the substance – and/or the behaviour – have become compulsive, with further loss of control and feelings of being unable to stop plus many rationalisations and excuses, as well as possibly grandiose or aggressive behaviour. The main carer becomes terrified by the aggression and is often increasingly withdrawn and silently angry, frequently attempting to control the compulsive behaviour by finding hidden supplies, trying to extract promises, lecturing and so on.

Then onwards and down, down, down through irrational thinking and possibly stealing to fund compulsive habits, the shakes, liver disease, mineral imbalances, psychological symptoms and physical consequences. Meanwhile, the main carer may develop stress-related symptoms until, as Wassner describes it, CAB *'hits bottom – use of substance / behaviour becomes an either / or choice. Next step – death or recovery.'*

The main carer also *'hits bottom, may leave addict, consider suicide. Or begin to recover.'*

Hopefully this 'hitting bottom' will lead to ... **coming up!**

'Breakthrough of denial, recognition of effects of addiction, admits the need for help to beat the compulsive behaviour ... and hope of change.' In Jay's case, that recognition of the effects of her very unhealthy eating patterns, and her acceptance that she needed some help to beat the compulsive need to control her food intake, were indeed the major turning points.

Whatever the life-affecting consequences of our choices, whether positive or negative, change is recognised to follow the same pattern as in other areas of life.

Stages of change

Precontemplation	– not really ready to change
Contemplation	– thinking towards change
Preparation	– gathering oneself
Action	– making the change
Maintenance	– following through.......
Relapse	– didn't make it this time, try again....

Recognising these stages in motivation can give carers, both home and professional, important clues as to how best to offer support.

In the face of Compulsive Addictive Behaviour (CAB)

The home carer's job is to offer support in the process of positive change (while living through the down times, acknowledging rather than ignoring them); to encourage and give confidence that change is possible; and calmly and quietly show confidence that the individual can, *with the right effort,* cope with change.

Remember: it is simply not possible to *make* someone change, unless they themselves recognise the need for change. However, it is possible, by gentle warmth and strong, calm encouragement, to help someone make positive changes in their own life.

Practical activity

Think of someone you know well.

Think of one aspect of their behaviour which has a negative impact on their life, from something relatively small to a major problem affecting many life areas – e.g. a lack of exercise, smoking, alcohol problems, overwork, an unhealthy diet.

Look again at the Stages of Change above.

Think of each stage in relation to your Person with the Problem.

With each stage in mind, make a list of the negative behaviours; e.g. precontemplation – lack of recognition or acknowledgement of negative impact of own behaviour; denial (often fierce) of problems.

What helped – or might help – motivate a change towards more positive behaviour?

What definitely did not help, and still does not help?

What 'Toolkit of Information and Resources' helped, or might have helped?

What led to, or is now leading to, maintenance of the more positive behaviour?

What led to/leads to relapses into former negative behaviour(s)?

Now: apply the Stages of Change to a more current problem.

***

My notes from Gill Todd's conference workshop for home carers

(Although Gill, a recently retired Clinical Nurse Leader at the Maudsley Hospital, London, was talking about eating disorders, the same ideas can be applied to other conditions.)

The aim of the workshop: to explore and resolve ambivalence towards changing behaviour which is having a damaging effect on health. *'Family and friends can play a vital role in showing that all-essential encouragement, warmth and caring support.'*

Suggestions for carers	*Try to avoid*
* be as warm and caring as possible	§ lecturing, arguing
* let him or her explain her arguments for change or for staying the same.	§ assuming authoritarian role § assuming expert role
* focus on his/her concerns	§ ordering, directing, threatening
* stress *choice* and responsibility	§ doing most of the talking
* discuss the pros and cons of choices	§ getting into debates about labels
* repeat and reflect what you feel s/he means	§ making moral statements
* summarise periodically	§ criticising, preaching, or judging
* admit when you make mistakes	§ asking three questions in a row
* avoid saying BUT....	§ outlining what YOU think is the problem
* be prepared to talk about your own role	§ prescribing solutions
	§ attempts to persuade with logic

Plus:
- Admit when you've made a mistake. If *you* can admit that you've been wrong, it could help make your loved one feel better about admitting to mistakes they've made. *Sorry –* the biggest word in the world?
- The carer's job is to support through the process of change, to encourage and give confidence that change *is* possible, that the individual *can* cope with change.

Rather than trying to 'set up' a discussion, try to find times to talk when the atmosphere is relaxed, perhaps when just sitting around, e.g. on a Sunday morning, or when out for a walk.

Be prepared to *listen to* rather than talk at.

Be prepared for a long road with two steps forward and one back, sometimes even several back, before renewed progress.

As on all long journeys, look out for support, look after yourself, give yourself breaks: a carer is there when no-one else is left. Always remember – *people change only when they themselves recognise, and accept, the need for change.* Remember the story of the battle between the sun and the wind to get a man to take off his coat? The sun smiled and shone gently and warmly – and the man at last recognised that he really needed to change.

And remember the stages of change? Precontemplation, Contemplation, Preparation towards personal change, Action and making those changes, Maintenance and following through.

But also sometimes Relapse – *didn't make it this time? Don't give up, try again.*

Janet Treasure notes in her article *Ready, Willing and Able to Change: Motivational Aspects of the Assessment and Treatment of Eating Disorders*[2] that assumptions made about the intentions of each party – health professional and patient – may be very different. The health professional may wish to offer clear strategies to help a patient, while the patient may only be there to please her distraught family and without any real interest in changing her self-destructive behaviour.

An imbalance of intentions can be present in compulsive/addictive conditions – and in other health problems too – and can cause huge frustration not only for family and friends but also for treating professionals, who walk a delicate tightrope between calmly offering acceptable options to their patients, mindful of all the possible consequences of alcohol or drugs or gambling, self-starvation or any other compulsive behaviour, and the awareness that the individual may give answers which they feel will please rather than with any serious intention of following through. Alternatively, perhaps the same individual leaves an appointment full of good intentions which evaporate on leaving the clinic.

Note the *gradual progression* towards any real change, rather than a quick decision followed by immediate and sustained positive action; setbacks are common on the long road to recovery. Also, the fact that 20% of patients with AN were in the 'Precontemplation' phase (in other words not really willing to accept the need or possibility of changing, no matter how much family and friends plead or argue or persuade), 30% were in the 'Contemplation' phase, leaving fewer than 50% in the 'Action' stage of change.

Motivating Alco – or Druggie, or Anorexia, or Gambo or whoever – towards positive change is one of the main areas where family/friends/carers can really help. *But they have to know what to do.* Feelings of helplessness and despair are common in the face of a loved one's dramatic personality change. Aggression and deceit, manipulation and low self-esteem are all part of the dark world of Alco or Druggie, where s/he believes no-one cares, s/he sees criticism at every turn, and no matter what people say or do in their efforts to help, s/he still believes s/he is unworthy of real love. Anything that just might prove otherwise is simply dismissed.

'Client resistance rates rose when a confrontational therapeutic style was used, and fell with a "client-centred approach".' How does this apply to carers? The benefits to patients of trying to increase confidence in their abilities to cope – again, how can home carers help with this? Without professional training, is this possible? ***Yes!***

'A good motivational therapist was able to (1) Understand the other person's frame of reference. (2) Express acceptance and affirmation. (3) Filter the patient's thoughts so that motivational

statements are amplified and non-motivational statements dampened down.' Again, praise anything positive, while simply noting rather than ignoring the negative.

I understand that the music for the well-known song *'Accentuate the positive...',* which was published in 1944 and has been recorded by many well-known singers and musicians, was written by Harold Arlen, with lyrics by Johnny Mercer – who told a 'Pop Chronicles' radio documentary that his inspiration was a sermon he listened to by Father Devine, with the subject *'You got to accentuate the positive and eliminate the negative.'* On hearing this, he said, *'Wow, what a colourful phrase!'*

How can carers apply this very sensible approach in a tough home situation?

Reactions in a fraught and frazzled situation

Reasoned argument? In my own situation when Jay was so ill, efforts to get Anorexia to change her eating habits by reasoned argument were more likely to drive Anorexia even further into her dark world where food was seen as the enemy. In fact, anything at all – a word or even a look, intentional or inadvertent – which might possibly be taken as criticism was picked on and exaggerated, with the most trivial incident built up by Anorexia into a reason for yet another extreme 'Hairy Jamaica'.

In many – most? – situations, in the long run biting back cross words in retaliation is much more effective than responding in kind, which will probably spark off yet another row.

Don't ignore the negative. Easy to say ... read on for how therapists cope with refusal to follow practical suggestions.

Try to have a calm comment ready for just such an occasion: by simply ignoring rudeness or any other negative behaviour, you risk endorsing it as acceptable. Again, try saying, *'I love you very much but I really don't like it when you...'* shout at me, slam doors, or whatever. *'Let's talk about ... when you're feeling better.'* Be prepared to repeat as necessary.

Have an activity lined up for after you've said your piece, e.g. *'Now I'm going out to walk the dog.'* As always, Dog will be pleased! Or perhaps you have urgent tasks to complete in your 'workroom' – or something else.

'*What seems to drive therapists into being confrontational is either the therapist's anxiety about the patient's physical state, frustration about the patient's lack of change, or disappointment and angry incredulity when faced with the patient manipulating their weight,*' writes Professor Treasure – which could also be said for trying to support and treat *anyone* who cannot or will not acknowledge the seriously negative effects of their behaviour. This is even more true for home carers, who daily see their loved one deliberately engaging in negative behaviour with potentially devastating effects.

Actively look for the positive

Praise whenever it is due, whether for small efforts or huge, can be a great motivator. Actively look for situations, efforts and behaviour you can honestly praise. As with all human beings, Anorexia, Alco, Druggie and Gambo (and all their friends) need the reassurance of love and acceptance, most especially when self-esteem is low. They may quite possibly recognise the effects of their behaviour – although they may not yet be ready to acknowledge that.

Giving praise in daily life?

No matter how much we may feel them inside, the words '*I love you*' may be rarely spoken as people struggle to cope with everyday commitments. Or '*I really like it when you...*' When did you last praise the positive, or say those special words '*Well done! It's great that you...*' to a family member, a special friend, a helpful neighbour, a valued colleague?

In our house, after several years of Bulimia regularly clearing the cupboards of all food I noticed the beginnings of improvement, and I commented on it. '*I can see you're trying hard – I know how difficult it is to beat your illness, I really appreciate your efforts.*' Jay was really pleased that I'd actually noticed – and redoubled her efforts.

For most people, although they might appreciate being told about your good feelings towards them, your words are a small added pleasure. However, for anyone experiencing mental distress, they can be really, *really* important. Gambo's hair looks good? *Say so*. That colour suits Alco? *Say so*. You've noticed that Bulimia has made an effort? *Say so*. No matter how small it may seem to you, perhaps even something which in the past would be taken for granted, such as leaving your favourite biscuit in the tin for you or making a cuppa for others, *note the effort and thought behind it, and say you've noticed and are pleased.*

Try to work out ways of giving options

For instance, in our house when Anorexia gained the upper hand, '*All breathing creatures have to eat. We breathe, therefore we must eat. Soon we're going to cook our meal –* **what** *would you like to eat?*' No comments on what she put on her plate – eating anything is better than eating absolutely nothing. Whatever the condition, keeping him or her alive is the aim of the home team until he or she accepts professional help and/or is motivated to change unhealthy habits – Alco to change his drinking, or Druggie her use of drugs, or Gambo his visits to the betting shop...

Talk about and emphasise memories of when your loved one coped well in a situation

Remind him or her that s/he could cope then and you're sure they will cope again just as well. (See also Chapter 6, *Communication*.)

Change rarely ever happens overnight ... don't give up

As always, hindsight is a wonderful thing. I look back on those years of blundering about without information and finding out by trial and error – loads of errors! – and I can see what really worked to help my daughter towards positive personal change. Would her recovery have come sooner if I'd found relevant information and support at the beginning of that long journey? I'll never know; I can only be thankful for somehow finding a way through.

Choosing the right words

As already outlined, most individuals not only have to perceive personal benefits but also to be convinced that they can follow through on the effort needed. Close family and friends can play a crucial role here in building – or blighting – motivation...

R had worked hard, felt that he had built up knowledge and experience as well as good relationships, and was now considering applying for further training towards future job prospects and possible promotion. His application was written and ready to post, all he needed was a stamp. Before he'd got around to buying the stamp he met his father. When R told his father what he was planning, his father's response was 'What makes you think you're good enough to go any further? Be realistic!'

And despite the encouragement of others, R quietly forgot about the application.

L

With just a few negative words, R's motivation and decision changed. With just a few different words, R's working – and possibly personal – life might have followed a different path.

These few words – careless and damaging, or helpful and motivating – may be from anyone, even occasionally from a casual conversation with someone at a bus stop or met on a train. When supporting a vulnerable individual it is even more important to choose those important encouraging words carefully. *In everyday life, it may not be possible to calmly evaluate every single word for possible adverse reactions – but simply being aware of other people's feelings, and making a conscious effort to 'praise the positive', is a very good beginning.*

'What resources will I need if I'm going to change?'

Exploring possibilities and resources – physical and emotional, plus determination and guts to follow through with a personally-difficult course of action – is another step towards motivation which close contacts can sometimes help with.

Offers of active help may be valued and accepted

Would you like me to come with you to the doctor / clinic / therapist?
I've found this interesting website / article / book – you might like to have a look at it.

No interest? Move the discussion on; don't try to 'persuade' and possibly set up resistance.

Let them go it alone?

Sometimes we have to step back. Trying to do everything for a loved one, rather than helping and supporting them to try things themselves, may smother initiative. Rather than build or rebuild confidence, it may convince them they can't achieve anything themselves, thereby taking away even the opportunity for personal growth. Meeting and tackling setbacks, making mistakes and learning from them, are all part of personal growth and the important yet delicate process of recovery. Judging *if* as well as *when* to step in – or whether simply to be there alongside if things go wrong – can be difficult, especially because at the 'Precontemplation' stage they may not be ready to contemplate change at all.

Whatever your own situation, a considered mix of different approaches at different stages of the journey, explored through home team discussions, can be tremendously beneficial in sharing the load as well as in developing a co-ordinated approach. (See Chapters 5 and 6, *Family Teamwork* and *Communication.*)

Active encouragement

Trying for consistent calm and encouragement is always important, especially when the going gets tough and the temptation to revert to former patterns is strong. That encouragement may be through:

- hugs and kisses
- smiles and obvious pleasure at success in following through on more acceptable behaviour
- simple spoken words – *I knew you could do it!*

- a written and tangible reward through a card or letter – *I'm so proud of you!* A card or letter has the added bonus of being kept to treasure and remind of success ... which may lead to further encouragement and motivation
- a treat or gift – no matter how small
- distraction when needed – a walk, playing a card or board game, sharing a film or TV programme
- reassurance that any setback does not inevitably mean the end of the battle
- encouragement to keep trying.

Sometimes progress is achieved through a long series of small steps forward interspersed with minor or major setbacks. Sometimes a plateau seems to be reached, with no more progress for some time. Sometimes sudden regression to a much earlier stage shatters carers' dreams of positive change ... at least for a while.

However, occasionally the beginnings of real work by the vulnerable individual may come unexpectedly and for unforeseen reasons. A major turning point in our house came like this.

Christmas and other festivals, with lots of food around and everyone else appearing happy and relaxed, can be difficult for many individuals for a variety of reasons, including for anyone with an eating disorder – and 1999 was the worst ever in our house, with several 'Hairy Jamaicas' exhausting everyone.

After over five years of struggle I'd reached breaking point. I said that perhaps if Jay didn't like living with me, objected to the house rules which were for everyone and not just her, perhaps she should look for somewhere else to live. She stormed out of the house threatening suicide.

As I waited, and waited, I wondered how I could possibly cope if she followed through on her threat. Eventually the dog raised her head and listened to quiet footsteps going upstairs. Jay was back. After asking what she had taken, I rang the doctor who reassured me that Jay would sleep off the effects.

Two days later I repeated what I'd said during our most recent confrontation – how much I loved Jay, how hard I'd tried to help and support her – and said again that I couldn't accept such behaviour in my own house, which I wouldn't accept from anyone else.

And two days further on again, Jay told me that she'd decided that perhaps she needed professional help after all. The wait for an appointment was agonising – would Jay change her mind? No. Over the next two years Jane, a specialist dietician, helped Jay to bring her eating under control during monthly appointments.

However, as in so many situations there were no guarantees anywhere along the line.

Treating professionals often feel frustrated when faced with a lack of motivation, a lack of progress – and for family members it is very painful as well as frustrating. This is where love can be a handicap. As professionals with long years of training have told me, when one of their loved ones and their own family are affected by a difficult health condition, all that training may not be much help. It is much more difficult then to remain calm and detached when you love the person destroying their own life.

I still wonder if I'd had some relevant information at the start of Jay's illness about common patterns and behaviour in eating disorders and how to try to help my beloved Jay – would the path of her illness have been different? Could it have saved her at least some of the misery and pain she went through? Would her struggles to beat those twin demons A and B have been shorter? I'll never know. I can only be thankful every day for her sustained recovery.

How long?

Whatever the long-term health problem, *change is unlikely to happen overnight* – especially when the behaviour has become ingrained over years, brain patterns have been worn to a groove and habits become entrenched by repetition of the behaviour many, many times.

There are no guarantees, ever.

The longer the timescale involved before tackling the problem, the more difficult the change to more positive behaviour; the more time and effort are required against the temptation to revert. All this must happen before any individual can feel they have beaten it. Even then, awareness and vigilance are needed to ensure that a recurrence is not triggered by future personal stress.

Family and other home carers should prepare for a long road – see Chapter 10, *Carer Survival*. Anything less can then be seen as a major bonus.

Notes

1   Wassner, A. (1990) *Recovering Together – how to help an alcoholic without hurting yourself.* An Owl Book.
2   Treasure, J. (2001) *Ready, Willing and Able to Change: Motivational Aspects of the Assessment and Treatment of Eating Disorders.* Online library, wiley.com (Accessed on 15/5/2014).

9

Information and Resources

Whatever the task we face in life, having relevant, practical basic information and resources – or not – can make or break the outcome. *Whatever* the situation – e.g. in a school, in an operating theatre, at home, travelling abroad, in an interview – accurate and adequate resources including relevant information *(What? Who? When? Where? How?)* are crucial to how that situation develops.

To gain an accurate picture of the individual lives of the people they work with, the problems within those lives and the special help needed, everyone involved in 'the caring professions' – including nurses, doctors, surgeons, psychiatrists, mental health nurses, teachers, Special Educational Needs (SEN) teachers, social workers, community workers – need as much accurate and relevant information as possible. Just imagine the chaos if all these people had no relevant training, information or other resources for their work!

For caring in a home situation, exactly the same is true: to enable them to complete the circle of care, family members and close others also need relevant information in their toolkit of resources.

'If only I'd known...' Just a few real-life examples of what can happen through lack of relevant information:

Following being taken into foster care, P had to change school. On his first Friday there he brought with him, in his new school bag, shorts and a tee-shirt to change into for PE. But when it came to time to change, P refused to get changed and became very distressed when he was encouraged to do so, preferring to sit out and watch the other children at games. Later his foster mum came to school to explain why P didn't want to take his shirt off: his back and arms were covered with marks where his father had often stubbed cigarettes out, despite his mother's attempts to protect him. If only I'd known right at the beginning about P's early experiences – I could have suggested he wear a long sleeved tee-shirt and loose trousers rather than the regulation kit, and saved P distress about his scars being visible and questions from other children, not to mention the reminders of a painful past.

Lesley

My uncle had a hip replacement operation, and was told he had to wear elastic stockings after the op. He hated them, said they were so tight they were really uncomfortable. When he got home, still wearing the stockings, he felt they were unhygienic after wearing them since the hip operation about ten days before. He also found it very difficult to remove them before having a bath, and then it was even more difficult to get them back on again. So he decided to take them off two weeks after the operation, and stopped wearing them.

If only he'd been told he had to wear them for much longer, and understood why, maybe he'd have seen a reason to keep on wearing the things, could have got an extra pair to make hygiene easier.

If only ... well, things might have been different, he probably wouldn't have landed back in hospital.

Frances

It's not possible to anticipate all problems. Many unexpected reactions are triggered by individual experiences, by differing understanding or interpretation. However, the more relevant the information and resources available and the better the communication, the easier it will be to avoid at least some difficult and possibly distressing – even tragic – situations.

Months into her illness, when Jay fell downstairs I helped pick her up and comforted her. Then it happened again. Both times she was bruised, and the second time she also twisted her ankle – and she brushed off any further attention. *'Stop fussing, Mum!'*

And then it happened again.

'It's like doing a jigsaw blindfolded...'

If only I'd been told that potassium deficiency is a common side-effect of disordered eating which can lead to heart failure, and if I'd known how to recognise the symptoms – which include difficulty climbing stairs – I'd have contacted the doctor for advice.

Practical activity – daily life

Choose any of the activities below.

- at home, the old heating boiler has broken down in freezing cold weather
- at work, the main central heating system has broken down
- your family want to go camping for a week
- you decide to redecorate your kitchen
- at work, essential supplies have not been delivered when promised

- due to severe arthritis, a family member can no longer get into the bath
- the washing machine has broken down
- your neighbour's tree has blown down across your garden
- the car needs servicing before its annual road test
- you have been asked to organise a family/school/community reunion or celebration.

Or perhaps you might think of a current situation you're tackling, or which you know you'll have to cope with in future.

Make some notes about what you would need to enable you to deal with any (or each) of the above situations.

If a situation changes from day to day – few situations remain static for long – what then?

Now – test yourself. What information would you need in the situation below?

Aunty Kath, now in her later years and not always in the best of health, wants to visit her daughter who lives in Australia. En route she also wants to visit the Japanese prison camp where her late husband was held during WW2. To make the most of the trip, Aunty Kath decides to invite some family members to help organise the venture and accompany her on the trip. Make some notes about what you might need.

What resources will be needed for this once-in-a-lifetime trip? For instance, travel information regarding flights/ships/buses/hire cars? Dates and times? Information on suitable accommodation in the places you'll visit? Information on when it is possible to visit the prison camp? What about currency while you're away, and the estimated costs involved in accommodation? The availability of medical care if needed? Medications possibly needed for the journey, any inoculations needed beforehand? Anything else?

Back to basics

Each situation can develop in so many ways. It may bring closure, or it may be the beginning of a whole new situation, may result in unexpected individual consequences ranging from hilarious, happy, loving and good to extremely difficult or awful, may affect one person or several, or even a very large number of people.

In *any* situation – whether work, home or social – *HOW* is it possible to work out what steps are needed to organise most effectively?

This is my own list:

- Assess the current situation – who is involved, who is affected?
- Assess how this situation currently affects you and others, or how it may affect you and others in the future.
- Assess all relevant factors – for instance, is this a new or lingering situation; is it short-term, or could it be long lasting with a wide range of possible further problems?
- Work out what resources are needed – e.g. any special equipment, finance to keep the household running, pay the mortgage or rent, buy clothes and shoes etc.
- What problems may be encountered? Differing tastes, views, attitudes, opinions?
- What information and resources will everyone need to make effective decisions? How can you ensure they each have what they need?
- Work out the best way of finding the relevant information, e.g. books, websites, charity information leaflets, local services, telephone directory. Do you need to check the legal situation, or insurance?
- How will you ensure everyone, including yourself, will have the right individual support?
- Can you make contingency plans for any possible future problems?
- Anything else you can think of?

Whatever the situation, a lack of relevant and accurate information can lead to unforeseen consequences, even to tragedy. In home care, for instance, the wrong dosage of medicine, infection due to negligent hygiene, accidents, depression, suicide, violence to self or others, rows because of misunderstandings, differing perceptions and assumptions … all of these are possible when trying to 'work in the dark'.

Information – WHO?

As noted earlier, over recent years there has been a sea change in attitudes. Research relating to building more effective 24/365 all-round collaborative care has shown that such collaboration can lead to higher recovery rates.

For instance, the *UK Department of Health New Horizons Consultation* (2009),[1] states very clearly: *'Providing inform-ation to service users and their families is an essential element of a care plan.'* This includes information about e.g. their health problem, the choices they have, the staff who will be providing care treatments and possible side-effects, available services, and, where relevant, the person's rights under the relevant Health Act. This can be provided as an 'information prescription'.

There are now many other recent publications, consultations, research and reports which acknowledge the importance of sharing appropriate information with home carers, and which endorse relevant changes in policy – e.g. the Mental Health Commission, New Zealand (1998),[2] the Department of Health and Human Services, United States (2003),[3] the Australian Government (2003)[4] and the Mental Health Commission, Ireland (2005).[5] Across the world, the crucial part played by home carers and close others is now being recognised.

Books too, including some textbooks, have begun to reflect this major change of tone. Robert S. Mendelsohn's *Confessions of a Medical Heretic*, published in 1979[6] and which I found last year in a second-hand bookshop, was one of the first and a revelation to me.

Also, very recently in a local library, I had more revelations when I found two books written and published in more recent years: *Models of Madness* edited by John Read, Loren R Mosher and Richard P Bentall,[7] and *Mad in America: Bad Science, Bad Medicine, and the Enduring Mistreatment of the Mentally Ill* by Robert Whitaker.[8] This last one had reviews stating that it was *'well-researched'*, *'a haunting history'* and *'mandatory reading for psychiatrists'*.

In the UK, great efforts are now being made in all areas across health and welfare systems to create official help for vulnerable people and their home carers. However, in some cases there still seem to be huge gaps in the provision of 'information prescriptions', let alone help with practical resources.

So – why are there still so many road-blocks in the system?

For instance, just one story of scrambled communications:

I've been sent a copy of my own 'Single Shared Assessment' – sixteen pages of notes on me as part of the current government survey of everyone claiming support from the government due to incapacity. My name is on the form ... but I don't recognise many other 'facts' given about me. In different parts of the form, my wife is referred to as my 'partner', with a different name given; the wrong phone number is quoted; dates given are wrong (starting in 1900!); my sex is given as female; the name of my doctor is wrong ... and several references are made to this woman – whom I understand died in this property, aged ninety-six.

My original injury from the accident at work is not noted, although Rheumatoid Arthritis is quoted as a disability – which I later developed, triggered I understand by my injury.

In my case, the Single Shared Assessment form seems to have got mixed up with someone else's details. So, when I answer their questions, my answers are different from the answers they already have on 'my' form. No-one seems interested in what I'm telling them.

And what if decisions are made based on what is currently on 'my' form?

Volunteering work is a survival technique for me – I often see others worse off than myself, and I do everything I can to help them. Gives a different perspective.

But trying to get help – filling in forms just to help us survive – when it seems my name has been somehow put on someone else's records, then updated occasionally under my name; there are several references to 'Mary' – and my wife has answered phonecalls at home to someone asking for 'Mary'.

No-one told me about the long term – at first I thought I'd be back at work in a few weeks! Fourteen years on, I have constant pain, twenty-four hours of every day. Mornings and nights are worst; I can't bear anything on my legs; I need help in dressing; I can't write properly because of nerve damage which means no hand control; and I can't lift my arms. I've suffered spells of depression and even thought of topping myself.

My wife is a great support to me – some people reckon I shouldn't get any other support or help – 'She's your wife, isn't she?'

And when I tried to ask about this, about how to get help to survive, to pay for our food and rent, I couldn't get anyone to listen to me, they just don't seem to believe me or think it's important. We can't survive without help, what are we going to do?

L, personal interview

Technology can bring great benefits, but when systems don't work properly it can also cause huge problems. Unfortunately in *any* situation, human error can occur, and the bigger the situation and the more people involved, the greater the possibility of mistakes. Files can somehow become mixed up, as in L's case above. Unfortunately there is often little or no contact or communication, let alone co-ordination, between all the health departments and specialists who may be involved with one patient, or when a computer-generated questionnaire is used without thought to individual variations in any particular condition or situation.

In the UK, ATOS[9] – which, according to its website, is *'an international information technology services company with annual revenues (2012) of EUR 8.8 billion and 77000 employees in 47 countries'* – has been contracted to assess all claimants for disability benefits since 2005. Using computer-generated questionnaires, ATOS assessors have been accused of rarely making eye contact with the patient, and of taking no account of facts such as the wide range of outcomes for the same disease, or the intricacies of mental illness. For instance, one question that is asked of everyone being assessed is: *'Can you pick up a pencil?'* This is regardless of whether their diagnosis is terminal cancer or bipolar disorder, or, as in L's case quoted above, the result of severe injuries due to an accident while at work on an oil rig. L's answer to that question would be: *'Yes, I can pick up a pencil – but I can't do much writing at all due to the nerve damage in my hand.'*

As Zoe Williams points out, *'the analysts have only six weeks' training in 'disability analysis', and are not required to be experts in the field of the illness in question. Yet their opinion takes contractual priority over that of the patient's consultant. Additional ongoing problems are frequently triggered for those with long-term medical conditions – some of our community's most vulnerable members – by these detached computer-generated questionnaire assessments rather than human beings professionally trained in health service.'*[10]

An outstanding example of the **lack of** anything which could be called 'Teamwork'?

Why the lack of relevant information? Shame and Blame theories – the long-term consequences

Unfortunately long years of finding blame within families, and treating the patient as completely separate from his home life and community, have meant that many professionals have little or no knowledge of the difficulties home carers may face.

Change and re-focus on collaborative care – HOW?

Carers play an important role in many service users' lives. Their knowledge and expertise represent an enormous resource for statutory and voluntary mental health services. These are reasons why it is so important to include them through sharing information.

Sharing mental health information with carers: pointers to good practice for service providers.

From NHS Continuity of Care, 2006[11]

Also, as Dr Mike Slade states in *100 ways to support recovery*:[12]

Working in a recovery-oriented way starts with a consideration of value. What are the guiding values of a recovery-oriented mental health service...? They don't have to be complex. Bill Anthony has proposed – 'People with severe mental illnesses are people.'

At last – common sense! There is now widespread recognition that people experiencing mental health (or any other) problems are simply human beings – *people!* – who need extra help and support from all the important people in their lives to help them cope with whatever life has thrown at them. *They are not just a collection of symptoms* – they are *people* from all sorts of different backgrounds, all ages and stages, all walks of life – *people* who are experiencing often-complicated problems in their own individual situation.

At last – this important and very welcome sea change has heralded the beginning of much more collaborative care.

It is distressing, therefore, and shocking, to read of official systems being used where decisions affecting many lives are being made on the basis of questions such as *Can you pick up a pencil?*

Finding relevant and accurate information and resources – where and how?

From treating professionals?

In some enlightened treatment services, information is already now offered by treating professionals to home carers, in leaflets and sometimes in the form of practical workshops.

Starting point?

As always, a good starting point is to ask treating professionals what help is available locally, what information they have about local self-help groups or charity organisations. Many health departments now have, or are developing, information booklets for those who need their help. For instance, recently an orthopaedic surgeon told me that he and his department are currently developing such a booklet for people having a hip replacement operation – and they have asked a patient to contribute. In some departments workshops have been developed to help carers provide home support – e.g. at the Maudsley Hospital Eating Disorders Unit.

And from other sources?

Friends and family – colleagues and acquaintances – book shops new and second-hand – libraries – websites – charity publications – magazine features – newspaper features – self-help groups – conferences – telephone help-lines – television programmes – radio programmes... In today's world, a huge range of possible sources of information exists. While finding them may be a little easier now than in past times, *it is very important to check for accuracy*. Research is continually growing, and as already noted in this book, some long-accepted theories – on which widely-promoted and used treatments were once based – have later proven to be inaccurate.

Just one example of major change...

In their 2008 book *Could it Be You?*, Dr Robin Pauc and Carina Norris[13] outline a revolutionary way of understanding dyspraxia, dyslexia, ADHD, OCD, autism and Asperger's Syndrome in adults – as symptoms rather than separate conditions, which, according to the new theory, are caused by the two sides of the brain being out of synch. Also according to this currently-developing theory, the symptoms may be treatable.

In his outline of the history of what were described as 'learning difficulties', Dr Pauc suggests that one of the two main parts of the brain fails to develop at the right time, possibly before birth.

He also outlines common delays in development in many specific life skills, a fact rarely noted when ADD, ADHD, OCD and autism were studied in isolation. This makes sense of observations often made by teachers in early-years education; e.g. when a child – let's call him John – who was identified in class as having difficulty in learning to read and write. John also found it difficult to organise, had difficulty in physical education and in getting dressed afterwards, was clumsy, anxious and easily distracted ... and was described often as 'disruptive' in a class of twenty-seven other pupils. Though this did not give a complete picture of the whole child and his difficulties, John was given a single specific label – ADD (Attention Deficit Disorder).

Considering John's difficulties as a whole – rather than concentrating solely on the formal educational subjects he found so difficult – the recent theories about developmental delays make more sense. Further research over coming years will no doubt lead to more clarification, development and adaptation of current approaches.

Therefore, whatever information and suggestions you find in your own quest, as always *it is extremely important to double-check and cross-reference with other sources, including the dates of publication, to ensure you have the most up-to-date information possible.*

How? Across the world there are now organisations – local, national, international – which exist to offer help, support and expert advice to home carers. For instance, in the UK there are many charity groups and organisations offering support for family and other home carers in all sorts of situations, all initially started by people whose vision included taking active steps to reach out and build much-needed support and offering a wealth of information and help. Local, national or international, wherever they are based, however they now operate, each of these organisations started when someone saw a need and tried to change things for the better. Some concentrate on the needs of people experiencing a particular condition, others offer help to individuals in a wide range of situations. (See *Carers' Resources*.)

Ask ... and go on asking

Whoever you ask for information, the person may not personally be able to provide the exact information you need, but they may be able to direct you to a source or put you in touch with someone who does know. Through this initial contact, they may possibly also help you to make contact with others with similar experiences who can share helpful ideas.

Support organisations – how a small acorn can grow into a mighty oak

Voluntary and charity organisations can often offer much-needed information and valuable support, having grown originally from a seed of recognition by one or two people of the help that may be needed in all sorts of circumstances – and how that help and support might be developed.

Just one acorn – the Aberdeen Association for Improving the Condition of the Poor – was formed in the late 1800s, later changing its name to the Aberdeen Association of Social Service in 1947 and becoming Voluntary Service Aberdeen from 1979 until 2006, when the title VSA was adopted.

VSA[14] has developed services for children, older people, adults with mental health problems and vulnerable families in Aberdeen and its surrounding area. It now employs over seven hundred staff. During its history the charity has been involved in the formation of several other organisations, including Aberdeen Citizens Advice Bureau, Aberdeen Children's Welfare Council, the Charities Aid Scheme, Easter Anguston Farm Training Scheme, the Aberdeen Volunteer Bureau, and the Aberdeen Carers Centre. Searching for information about just one organisation which can help you may lead to much more than expected!

Also, looking up just one website, Carers Trust[15] – a UK national organisation that was Crossroads Care and The Princess Royal Trust for Carers until recently – on the home page I found areas to be explored which lead to a great range of frequently-updated information relating to home care – *What is a Carer? Getting Help. Carers Chat. Money and Benefits. Local Support. News. Get Involved.*

(All voluntary organisations need volunteers with all sorts of personal experience to help in all sorts of ways – keeping records, answering the phone, supporting people who need help, keeping the accounts. Is there anything here that you could help with?)

The names above are only a very few examples of great oaks growing from tiny acorns. Finding out what exists in your own area could be the beginning of much more personal support.

Here is another very new idea – following what was seen as a successful experiment in Devon, a recent (2011) government-backed scheme is being developed: some supermarkets are coaching pharmacists and other workers in how to discreetly question those collecting prescriptions on behalf of others, or perhaps shopping with separate baskets, before directing them to in-store health professionals.[16]

Remember the old saying, *If you don't look, you won't find?* And then there's the one that says *The squeaky wheel is the one that gets oiled...*

Finance – and hard choices

Care and support are often very much linked to how resources are allocated, which varies from country to country and even region to region. In the UK there is a national health service funded by taxation, but the allocation of resources differs in different areas, depending on health authorities' priorities and decisions. For instance, in many areas provision for in-patient mental health conditions has been seen as a relatively low priority in comparison to physical conditions, and mental health services are often referred to as 'the Cinderella service' with relatively little funding allocated to these specialist resources.

In Scotland, for instance, until very recent years any specialist in-patient beds for eating disorders were provided in private nursing homes and paid for by the NHS. Even when someone was in a life-threatening condition, there was no NHS in-patient specialist care for eating disorders. If a local Health Board did not believe in funding treatment in a specialist private facility, possibly at some distance, the only other provision was in a general NHS ward with staff trained in nursing – but with no training specifically in eating disorders.

It was only in 2005, after a long campaign by home carers and professionals working together on a petition and with presentations by a team of the same professionals and carers communicating little-known facts to the Scottish Government Health Committee, that the very first specialist twelve-bed in-patient NHS ward was finally opened in Scotland – another good example of successful collaborative professional/home carer effort and teamwork.

Hard choices all round...

In many other countries, for instance USA, treatment is mostly dependent on adequate insurance. One American mum told me:

Our daughter is very ill, she needed treatment in hospital and was admitted some time ago as her condition was life-threatening – our doctor told us it was the best place she could be. At first she refused treatment but finally she agreed. It was very, very difficult, especially when she kept saying we wanted her in hospital because we didn't love her! It was just a nightmare ... in the end I think maybe she was really too tired to argue any more, she was like a skeleton and too weak to do anything but lie in bed. Anyway, over the last three or four months she's made some progress, and her attitudes seem to be changing.

But it's a very hard illness to treat and the specialist told us she'll probably need to be in there for quite a while, probably months, or she is likely to regress. Now the hospital has told us that our insurance will soon run out, can only fund her there for another few weeks. So if we can't pay for treatment, she'll be discharged. We're sick with worry, we've tried to work out what to do – we all think she should be in hospital. Should we sell our house to pay for her treatment? But if we do that, where will we live? My husband is getting really depressed, and I don't feel too good either. What are we going to do?!

E, personal contact

Many, many home carers, in all sorts of circumstances, find themselves with extremely hard choices:

My son N is 20, was really good at sport, very athletic and keen on the training he'd started to be a PE teacher. But since the accident he needs full time care – he needs help to get dressed, to fasten his clothes, to tie his shoes; help getting undressed, and help getting into bed at the other end of the day. Needs help to get to the toilet, or to have a shower, help to cut up his food, has huge difficulty getting upstairs.

He's really, really frustrated with the whole thing. I think he's depressed too. And no-one knows how long it might take for him to be any better. His friends have been very good, visiting him in hospital – but he hates needing help like he does now, hates them seeing him this way, hates having to ask for help.

J, his dad, works offshore, has done for years and he's away a lot. I've worked as a school admin assistant for the last ten years or so, and because we were both working and we were bringing in a goodly amount every month, we bought our own house. It's a lovely old house, four bedrooms, sort of rambling – but it needed a lot of renovation, needs a lot of maintenance. To pay for it all, we took on a mortgage – but it was great for the kids, especially the garden. We've still got twelve years to go now, before our mortgage is finished.

At least my son can sleep downstairs in his own room when he comes home – we put a bathroom in downstairs too. We feel one of us will have to give up work when our son comes home. I don't really want to give up my job; my husband quite likes the idea of being at home again, fancies starting his own business...

But – what happens if his great business idea doesn't work out and we can't make enough money to pay the mortgage and all the bills? We'd have to move into a smaller house, probably in a different area. Nobody in the family wants to move, and we really want our son living with us at home, it's what he wants too. And wherever he is, he'll need help, twenty-four-hour care. To stay here, keep on the mortgage and pay all the bills, we both really need to work. Or pay someone to be here when we're not. I just don't know what to do for the best.

P, personal contact

Although this is probably very different from your own situation, perhaps you can look at P's situation with more detachment and suggest what or who might help P and her family to cope with their very tough times.

One of several stories in his book *The Selfish Pig's Guide to Caring*, Hugh Marriott[17] writes about Clare who gave up her job to care for her husband Alun:

I had been given a pack for Disability Living Allowance[18] when Alun became entitled to Incapacity Benefit[19] – but binned it thinking that it didn't apply to him. I only applied thirteen months after the stroke, after Alun had been medically retired.

Clare eventually filled in the necessary forms, finding that it was more or less impossible to apply the questions asked to brain injury. Then she went to the Citizens Advice Bureau[20] who told her not to come back until the claim had been rejected three times! Only then, they said, could the decision be challenged. When a doctor eventually did see them, he would only speak to Alun. As Alun had limited insight into his problems at that point, it was only when Clare was allowed to explain Alun's difficulties that the doctor realised the extent of the effects of the stroke – and had to scrap his notes. Eventually, more than seven months after the claim, the DLA benefit arrived. As Clare said, it had been *a hell of a time*. No-one had explained Alun's eligibility for the DLA until Clare was encouraged to do so by a carer at the Princess Royal Trust. (For adults, DLA was changed in 2013 to *'Personal Independence Payment'*.[21])

Perseverance and patience are called for – to add to all the other attributes needed by family and other home carers. Therefore, for the sake of your loved one, and for you and your family – don't be afraid to look and to ask, to keep on looking and asking about what you need. Resources, including relevant information, may not be all you'd wish for, but if you don't at least try and try again to explore all possibilities, it's very unlikely that what is available will simply fall into your lap.

Notes

1   UK Department of Health New Horizons Consultation, 2009.
2   Mental Health Commission, New Zealand (1998) www.justice. govt.nz (Accessed on 15/5/2014).
3   Department of Health and Human Services, United States (2003) www.hhs.gov (Accessed on 15/5/2014).
4   Australian Government (2003) www.aihw.gov.au (Accessed 15/5/2014).
5   Mental Health Commission, Ireland (2005) www.mhcirl.ie (Accessed 15/5/2014).
6   Mendelsohn, R. (1979) *Confessions of a Medical Heretic.* Warner Books, USA.
7   Read, J., Mosher, L. R. and Benstall, R. (Eds) (2004) *Models of Madness: Psychological, Social and Biological Approaches to Schizophrenia.* Brunner-Routledge.

8 Whitaker, R. (2002, revised 2010) *Mad in America: Bad Science, Bad Medicine, and the Enduring Mistreatment of the Mentally Ill.* Basic Books, USA.

9 ATOS www.atos.net (Accessed 15.5.2014).

10 Williams, Z., *Guardian*, 29.12.11.

11 NHS Continuity of Care, 2006.

12 www.rethink.org (Accessed 15/5/2014).

13 www.barnesandnoble.com/w/could-it-be-you-robin-pauc/1115220 910?ean=9780753519066 (Accessed 20/6/2014).

14 www.vsa.org.uk (Accessed 15/5/2014).

15 www.carerstrust.org (Accessed 15/5/2014).

16 www.nhs.uk/Livewell/Pharmacy (Accessed 15/5/2014).

17 Marriott, H. (2003, reprinted 2004, 2006, 2007, 2008) *The Selfish Pig's Guide to Caring.* Sphere, UK.

18 Disability Living Allowance, www.gov.uk/dla-disability-living-allowance-benefit (Accessed 21/6/2014).

19 Incapacity Benefit, www.gov.uk/incapacity-benefit (Accessed 15/5/2014).

20 Citizens Advice Bureau, www.adviceguide.org.uk (Accessed 15/5/2014).

21 Personal Independence Payment, www.gov.uk/pip/overview (Accessed 15/5/2014).

10

Carer Survival

This last chapter tries to sum up what all family and other home carers need to survive.

The impact of caring

Whatever the illness or condition, long-term home caring can be difficult, exhausting, sometimes even frightening. The stress can have a major impact on the health of carers, possibly physical (e.g. palpitations, blood pressure problems, increased vulnerability to infection), mental (e.g. lack of concentration, anxiety, absent-mindedness), and emotional (e.g. feelings of failure, depression). People with little or no support in their long-term caring role are very vulnerable and can end up experiencing chronically low mood, or feeling constantly worried, irritable and easily annoyed, often doubting their ability to cope at all – and they may eventually collapse.

Many home carers, focused completely on the responsibility of supporting their loved one and believing that they must put all their own needs aside, often don't recognise signs of stress in themselves.

Unfortunately, rather than providing the best care possible, this complete focus on their loved one while ignoring their own needs can lead to a home carer's own health breaking down. If carers burn out completely, who will be there for their loved one?

Therefore it is *essential* that home carers consider their own lives and health, and what they themselves need to get through those tough times.

I too had to learn this lesson.

A struggle to cope

My own survival

Struggling daily to work out what was the best thing to do in difficult situations way beyond any of my previous experience, I too came very close to breakdown. I knew that I was so very tired and felt really unwell. At last, after making sure that friends would be around for my daughter, I arranged to attend a retreat weekend in peaceful surroundings (near home – just in case). Someone else would organise the meals and so on, there would be interesting activities during the day and pleasant company round the fire in the evenings. I would walk in quiet woods or on the beach, listen to the wind, breathe in peace. A little bit of heaven for two whole days.

On the first evening we all ate round the table, went to bed fairly early, and slept very well. I got up next morning for a relaxed breakfast at nine, went back to my room to read for a while before the first activity started at eleven ... and woke up just after four in the afternoon! Yes, I'd slept all day and missed all the planned activities. Vowing to do better next day, I went out for a long walk on my own, again enjoyed a pleasant evening meal, shared music and chat round the fire. Again I slept well, had breakfast at the same time, then returned to my room for a while before the first shared activity of the day... You're ahead of me? Yes, again I sat down. And again, I woke up in the late afternoon.

Although I'd missed most of the weekend's shared organised activities which I'd looked forward to so much, I felt the weekend had not been wasted – I'd learned a valuable lesson about just how completely exhausted I was, and that if I was to continue supporting and caring for my daughter, I really needed to plan for some personal breaks.

Mealtimes with Anorexia or Bulimia were rarely peaceful and often very difficult. So from then on, I arranged regular time out of the house every week for a meal; if no friend was free to share it, I went to a café and took a good book with me. Before I started I discussed my plan with Jay and each week I told her where I was going. I also suggested TV programmes or films she might like to watch, or friends or family members she might phone for a catch-up chat. I gave her a time when I'd be back, and I made sure that I returned on time.

In straightforward language, I also told her quietly but matter-of-factly *why* I was going to do this every week. '*I can see how difficult it is for you at mealtimes, but I find it really difficult to have all my meals with you just now – sometimes the anorexia or bulimia is really strong, and I can't relax. I worry about your health and what your illness is doing to your body. I love you so much, I really don't want to lose you, and to go on sharing the house with you, I need a break sometimes.*'

Although Anorexia and Bulimia initially tried hard to persuade me not to go out at all, Jay coped with my absence

– as I'd believed she would. By acknowledging my own need for a break and by following through on my plan, I not only gained time to recharge my batteries, but also helped to rebuild Jay's confidence that she could indeed again cope on her own.

Some common signs of stress

More irritation, arguments, disagreements and tension at home.

Less or no energy to enjoy long-standing hobbies and other activities.

No opportunity and no time to do things together with your family.

No time or energy to share time with other family members.

Less interest in sex.

Feelings of exhaustion.

Not finding time to socialise with friends.

Feeling distant from friends, avoiding meeting them.

Lack of interest in previously shared and enjoyed activities.

Reluctance to answer the phone or the doorbell.

Unable to concentrate, making more mistakes.

Less resilient when things go wrong.

Cancelling holidays or breaks, even short ones, away from home.

Lack of self-care or personal hygiene, wearing clothes for days without washing.

Letting things go – housework etc.

Leaving bills/correspondence unopened, or not replying due to lack of energy.

Deteriorating health. No time to go for check-ups, or to attend health appointments.

Perhaps you recognise aspects of your own life in the list above?

The choice

Carry on as you've always done? Or recognise how your responsibilities are affecting your own health? *Remember,* exhaustion and intense personal stress can – and unfortunately often do – lead to collapse.

Don't let yourself reach that stage, make a practical action plan.

One step at a time – how?

All action plans begin with a *first step*, in this case admitting how long-term care giving is affecting your health. This can be very difficult, especially if you're a person who likes to do their very best. It can also feel very hard to think of doing things for yourself when you feel your first priority should be caring for your loved one.

Start small?

Even ten minutes a day can make a difference – ten minutes of breathing space to think of what changes you'd like to make – and half an hour's breathing space may seem like a luxury. Remember, a luxury is something you don't really need. Remember also that rest and recharging those batteries is *essential* to ensure that you can continue caring most effectively.

Where? Those precious minutes need not always be outside your home. Perhaps you can identify a spare room, an attic or a shed which can be re-organised into a hobby room or a personal 'den', or a nearby quiet space in a local library or church, community or carer centre.

You've found space at home? Great!

Having a signal everyone knows can be another important step – a *Do Not Disturb* sign... My own was to go into my work room and close the door, which was usually open, after telling everyone about this signal. I found that simply sitting quietly, breathing slowly and deeply, helped. Or sometimes I stood and watched the birds outside. Soon I didn't need to actually mention *why* I was closing the door ... wonderful.

Gradually those initial precious ten minutes grew, and I could repeat them more often during the day. Later, as the time extended I'd go out for a walk with the dog or have a cuppa with a neighbour, or visit a friend, always letting Jay know where I'd be. Gradually her self-confidence that she could cope on her own returned.

Every situation will be different. Work out how *you'd* like to use some peaceful minutes, how to make those spaces of time a reality.

Next steps

Make a list of ideas. What would you really like to spend time on? Perhaps a hobby you've given up some time ago? Or try something new – e.g. drawing or painting, singing, listening to music, going to the cinema or theatre, go running, play golf, join a group with a common interest. You could explore reflexology, or reiki, tai chi or other relaxation techniques (all of which I explored over the years, and found very helpful in different ways). Perhaps look for a class, or a DVD or TV programme to help you. The choice is yours.

Remember – those small steps are important towards finding what *you* need to help you recharge.
Write down your plan of action – with details. For instance:

> *I will start introducing this change in my life on …* (choose a date, and a time)
> *To prepare for this change I will have to …*

Consider any obstacles which might hinder you in making the change. Perhaps someone may complain about your time being taken up rather than given to them? Or you may need to arrange for someone else to be with the vulnerable person at the centre of all your efforts? You may even feel guilty about wanting to follow your own interests and needs at all.

Think – what would a good friend say to you? What would *you* say to a dear friend? Perhaps: *'Everyone needs a break, a rest, to recharge their batteries. I get very tired sometimes – everyone needs a rest sometimes. And **you** need a break too.'*

Praise the positives

Note what went well, what happened, what you did, when and how – and why not give yourself a gold star? Yes, one good way to actively counter low self-esteem is to recognise, acknowledge and then write down incidents where you coped well and didn't crumble under pressure. For example: *I helped Mo with her homework while I was making tea. I remembered to order flowers for Mum's birthday even though there are so many other things to think about.*

Actively pay attention to those small things you achieve every single day. Remember to give yourself the same credit you award to other people.

Next steps?

When you recognise that one step has become established, begin to think about *what comes next* in developing and building your survival plan.

***

Resources, in addition to relevant information, often seem inadequate, rarely plentiful. In a perfect world, what would *you* put on your list to help you cope? Time? Accurate information? Accommodation? Energy? Equipment? Finance? Resilience to infection and personal illness? ICE (In Case of Emergency) plans? Anything else?

Now make your own list and discuss with your own home team or a close friend. *More than one meeting may be needed to give each topic enough time. How, as a team, can you build the best twenty-four hour care possible, taking into consideration the needs and feelings of everyone involved? This should include recharge-the-batteries breaks.*

A few things to consider for your list

Time – e.g. adequate time to spend helping and supporting the vulnerable individual. Time to spend on helping and supporting close others. Time to rest, refresh, replenish your own reserves. Time for activities outside the home.

Accurate Information – what do you need? As noted in the last chapter, *look* for what you feel you need – *and ask* your GP, or minister, friends, family members, other home carers.

Energy – carers need huge amounts of this! Energy is needed to give the much-needed support, physical and emotional, 24-hour/365 days a year. The needs of other family members still have to be considered, the household organised – home life, shopping, cooking, washing, cleaning, all need to continue.

Accommodation? While workplaces have usually been designed, chosen or adapted to suit the activities of those who work there, the work of home caring is frequently expected to be carried out without any regard to suitability of the venue. When someone needs special support at home, all sorts of facilities may become inadequate – for example, bathrooms, stairs, sleeping arrangements, laundry/washing, kitchen and living areas.

In most home situations, it is unlikely that the accommodation will be exactly what's needed for the change in daily life and needs. Again, ask your contacts if they can think of any way of making home life easier. Sometimes we get too close to a situation to be able to see other possibilities, such as installing extra shelving or individual cupboards. After discussion, maybe you could work out a rota for *everyone* in the household to help with chores. Rather than simply allocate all the tasks, ask which jobs each would like to volunteer for. Even young children can often help lay the table, count the right cutlery for places at the table – and often actually enjoy it, especially when they feel 'part of the team'.

Equipment – what would be ideal? Lifting and turning someone in bed; using the toilet; changing; bathing... Without the right equipment available, all these may become really difficult issues. Who might be able to help in your situation? In our area, the Occupational Therapy Department at the local hospital can arrange for such equipment – perhaps your doctor or local hospital can give you a contact.

Try to rearrange? While current home conditions may not be ideal, trying to rearrange the use of rooms may cause further problems for other family members who prefer the original arrangement. Equipment to help with physical problems, e.g. furniture added to the only bathroom for the household, may serve as a constant and unwanted reminder of changed days and responsibilities. If and when moving house, or if a rearrangement of room use is needed, a round-the-table discussion before the change is made could help avoid possible ill feeling – and give everyone an opportunity to discuss their feelings about the changes.

Finance – How is the household to continue to survive? The household still needs to function, pay its bills.

> *I really don't know what to do – last month I had to do the ATOS test, and when they asked me if I could hold a pencil of course I said yes ... I never thought that would mean to them that I can write a whole page, let alone take notes! I wish I could. I have constant nerve pain in my hands, even writing my name is a problem. Now they say I should be on a back-to-work programme. They just don't seem to believe me – or believe my doctor either! I used to have a good job, good friends, invited out a lot, went on holiday with the crowd.*
>
> *I've had to move back in with my mum too, I'm the only one living at home now. What happens if I get worse? She says she'll give up work, but how will we manage to pay the rent and food and heating?*
>
> *Thought I'd get married one day and have kids. Not now. I often feel like ending it all, it just goes on and on.*
>
> Barbara, personal contact

Work commitments – Often home carers have to make very hard choices. Continue to work or not? What are the consequences of these changes for other members of the family? If a carer has to give up paid employment to look after a loved one, *how* are the bills to be met? Who might be able to offer a detached view and practical suggestions for your/the household's financial survival? A good friend? A charity? A bank manager? A social worker?

ICE – *In Case of Emergency.* How to respond in various situations, how to recognise an emergency – these are very important topics for discussion for any home group. Just a few pointers for discussion:

- A list of useful numbers written clearly and posted next to the phone, including the mobile phone contact lists of everyone in the household.
- Discussion of what *might* happen in a 'worst case scenario', and what to do in these circumstances.
- Even young family members can be given a simple outline of what to do if, for instance, they notice someone fall down very suddenly – find an adult and tell them immediately what's happened. Talk about what they might say and how to tell e.g. a neighbour, a grandparent, an older sibling.
- Anything else which could be useful in case of emergency?

Thoughts about these discussions, and the possible need for such a list, may feel quite scary. Reassurance can also be given, that this is for the worst and most difficult scenario. Knowing what to do, and who to call for help, could be really important.

When everyone knows what just *might* happen – and the important part they can play – it can also be reassuring to know what is best to do.

The alternative is to ignore all such possibilities. Unfortunately, in some illnesses and conditions, this may lead to much worse difficulties and even tragedy. Better to be prepared and hope you'll never need to use the contents of such a list and discussions.

Resilience to infection and personal illness – Without respite and time to relax, carers also risk lowering their immune system and becoming less resilient to infection, as well as feeling exhaustion, isolation and depression. It is often easier to identify what's missing than to find it!

Quite apart from the actual hours given each day to your loved one, even working out how to organise all that you need in your situation can take up a lot of time and energy.

I didn't realise I'd given up so much in my own life – I used to play golf, sing in a choir, go to ballroom dancing classes, help with the local pantomime. Now the only time I'm out of the house is to take in the washing, or out for a quick run round the shops for essentials.

Mary-Ann

Perhaps you recognise Mary-Ann's situation – or maybe Pamela's:

One weekend my aunt came to stay here and I was able to go away to a carers' conference. When I came home, I felt able to cope again.

Pamela

Pamela has since talked to two friends about how she felt before and after her conference break – and they both said that they'd like to help. They also helped her to find out about local respite care provision.

You've made your list? Now, what next steps will you need to make it happen?

Some time to yourself? Being able to share concerns, as well as the happy times, with friends? Assertiveness training to help you cope with aggression? Fewer money worries?

Choose one item on your list

What resources do you need to make it happen?
Who could help you?
   Are there any of your friends or contacts who might be able to suggest your next steps? Contact a charity with experience of supporting families through difficult times? Is there a carers' centre near you? A doctor or social worker or your local authority who may be able to give you information about respite care in your local area?
Don't forget – in many countries, including the UK, there are now statutory rights for people who provide care at home, and local authorities are required to meet these statutory regulations.

Check the other items on your list

For each one, work out what you need to do to make them a reality. Tick them off as you follow your plan of action. Then, on to the next item.

Remember – as and when circumstances change, return to each topic on the list as necessary.
This is not easy when you're busy with your home caring role… Keep in mind that to allow you to continue giving that crucial care, time to plan ahead is not a luxury – it's *essential* to make sure you are physically and emotionally able to continue.

***

Notes, journals, letters, stories – any time, anywhere

Writing down feelings is a good way of dealing with them, helping to keep them in perspective and helping individuals cope, especially through tough times. I often wrote a page or two about what was happening at home – a sort of journal – and only later realised how much it helped me. Eventually I thought perhaps my experiences and notes about what I found helpful as a home carer might be useful to others, which led me to explore existing research and to interview other home carers.

Perhaps writing of your experiences may even be useful for people developing treatments. Most professionals have great qualifications, can quote lots of theories – but, apart from the few with personal experience, they often have little or no idea of behaviours outside the sheltered and structured environments of hospitals or clinics.

I now recognise writing as one of my main ways of getting through those difficult years. For me, writing (stories, poems, an occasional play) had always been a hobby, an interest, possibly to be developed one vague day in the future. I simply didn't anticipate that my writing would feel like a support to me as well as sometimes providing a bit of distraction during those long difficult years, let alone consider going on to develop it further. It would have been beyond my wildest dreams ever to imagine that I'd write non-fiction books published by a worldwide publisher, and be asked by Professor Janet Treasure to co-author another book with herself and Anna Crane, as well as this final non-fiction effort especially for home carers, many of whom have shared their experiences which I quote in their own words throughout this book.

Included in the many items I wrote during my own years of home caring was this: 'Her voice is gone'. Reading it brings back all my feelings at that time, of helplessness, complete despair and no-light-at-end-of-the-tunnel. Not only was Jay's voice obliterated by those twin demons, but my mother's gentle Irish voice too had been silenced. Following ten years of hearing only the frequently harsh and critical voice of Alzheimer's, sorting out my mother's belongings after her death I came across some letters and notebooks in her own handwriting which she'd written in much earlier times. Reading them through, I remembered her as she really had been – as my mother. I wrote a poem for her.

Her voice is gone

Her voice is gone, taken by the reaper.
I open the door, breathe the silence of the room,
remember spite, acid drops destroying
warmth, and love retreating
bewildered.

Your voice too, the gentle tones gone,
unrecorded, soft Irish words fading
into sweet memory. Then the phone rings,
brings it back through beat of pain. I hear again
my mother.

Today I opened the box and found
papers, jumble of papers carrying your thoughts,
papers with your hopes, dreams of peace,
visions for a world gone mad.
I sifted through the phrases, written as you
tried desperately to hold on, fight against
the void She brought. Each faded scrap, covered in your battle
for light, carried your voice, the words blurred
with loss.

In your mind God brought rest
to the weary, retribution to the wicked. Faded cuttings too,
treasured, kept for years against the dark. This one, clipped
onto your notes, gave plans, a peace accord. You wrote,
'Thank you, God'

for the peace you thought was coming then.
War would stop, men live as brothers,
the grief of centuries lift and clear. The world
would join voices, dance in celebration and all
would rejoice.

Years on, the world's still mad,
power rubs shoulders with greed, hatred
and despair. The noise of war shrieks loud
around our heads, gathering pace
unmindful.

Her voice is gone, taken by the reaper
flown with the crazy fray.
Your *words live on.*

Now, it is a constant joy to hear again Jay's own voice, and to remember my mother's own voice before Alzheimer's took over.

Beginnings in writing

From a very early age, even young children often find expressing their feelings on paper can really help – as well as being fun. They may give a name to a character they've drawn and then 'talk' as the character, explaining their feelings, or they may draw a picture and ask an adult to write their words on their drawing.

Keeping a journal, writing letters to real or imaginary folk, or developing stories from all sorts of incidents with real or imaginary characters – all these can be a great outlet for children and adults, especially in tough times. Creating a completely imaginary escape world can also be great fun, making unexpected things happen to imaginary characters. Some of these stories, characters, poems, plays, may later be turned into longer pieces.

Ceremonial shredding?

For very painful memories, even years after the event it can help to write them down in horrid detail and then have a ceremonial shredding, the paper and memories together shredded with a sense of relief and 'letting go'. Alternatively, if you have an open fire or wood burner, watch them go up in flames.

Sparky spelling – gruesome grammar?

Some folk worry about spelling or grammar, but here these are the very last things on the list. As a writer, it is up to you whether or not to share what you write with anyone else. It is only if and when you want to share what you've written with a supportive friend, or a local writing group, that spelling or grammar *might* matter.

Writing – or drawing – tools

- A notebook or writing/drawing pad is a good investment for scribbling or sketching ideas, thoughts and feelings, noting interesting people, comments, incidents and conversations, describing a room you're sitting in or a favourite place, what you can see from your window, a pet, unusual weather – anything you choose.
- Perhaps you know someone who could give you some sheets of A4 printer paper? Perhaps use the back of discarded sheets?
- Perhaps you have a computer, or could borrow one? Libraries often have computers for public use – and a quiet place to use them.
- I find a dictionary very helpful, and fascinating for finding new words; a thesaurus can be useful to find alternative words and phrases.
- Online spell checkers may also be useful for checking how to spell a new word you've heard.
- Libraries and bookshops can be a great source of helpful and practical books, including dictionaries and thesauruses, with assistants to help you find what you need.

A *journal* may be written every day, once a week or occasionally. It may be kept completely private, may be kept or destroyed, may be shared or not. Each entry may be a single sentence or paragraph, a page or several pages long; the same is true of sketches. The choice is yours.
Music can also affect all sorts of feelings. Depending on the piece of music and its style, as the voices and instruments express rhythm, soar and fall, leap and sway, many people feel the world fades as the music takes over, perhaps getting your feet tapping, your body moving. Music may bring joy and

pleasure, may bring sad memories or break and soothe a mood of sadness, help you express grief and pain.

Making music as well as listening to it can be enjoyed alone, or shared. Music can also be a great connector. Even when few words are spoken, sharing music – at home, at concert or club, in a choir or a group – can bring relaxation. Whether Country and Western or classical, pop, jazz or blues, traditional folk music or opera, music can bring all the feelings mentioned above. For many people, listening to, playing or dancing to music means complete concentration and forgetting the world outside. Afterwards there is a feeling of renewal, being more able to face whatever comes next.

Music may also have a good effect on mood. Experiment with different styles – peaceful and quiet or rousing and fun. Who knows, you may find another way through some very difficult times, a way of calming difficult or troubled feelings – your own as well as others, including those of the vulnerable person at the centre.

Walking, biking, swimming, yoga, tai chi, aerobics and other exercise

These too can bring some release and relaxation. Finding space in your caring duties, and someone to be there in your absence, may prove difficult – but it is well worth exploring to allow you to recharge your batteries.

Think: Who can you talk to, tell how you're feeling, ask to help you find support?

Isolation – how do other people cope?

As always, there are individual differences. Some seek a solitary life, while others want company at all times. Most of us are somewhere in the middle, enjoying the company of friends and family most of the time while also valuing spells of solitude or 'peace within company', when a group of people share an activity involving others but without expectations of closeness – whether it is knitting, drawing, upholstery, bowling, cooking or yoga, joining a group with a common interest can give very welcome spaces in the seemingly-relentless process of providing long-term care.

Change and individual choice

Many human beings find it difficult to cope with prolonged distance from their family and friends, whatever the reason or life circumstances. Even joyful changes such as getting married or the birth of a longed-for new baby, and positive changes such as starting a great new job, may cause individual stress.

This is much more difficult when a loved one's life changes without choice through unhappy circumstances, and the changes bring struggle and sadness in our lives. When a loved one has need of extra ongoing support and care, family members and friends have a choice: try to offer our individual best, or...?

I know one person whose husband had a severe stroke and right from day one she just couldn't cope. She went to see him in the hospital that first day, said she couldn't do it. She just walked out and never went back.

Alexis

But very few walk away. Most people taking on a home care-giving role don't even consider any possible consequences for themselves; even if and when they *do* realise that their own lives have been significantly affected, most home carers quietly continue with their home care role, often coping with great personal stress.

Sometimes that stress may be eased by being able to share it with close family and friends who are willing and able to help. In some circumstances more peace and quiet is needed.

It came as a huge shock when R was diagnosed with terminal cancer and given weeks rather than months or longer to live. Everyone wanted to help and rallied round – his wife and children, his relations and many friends, colleagues and neighbours; everyone wanted to help in any way they could. The doorbell – and the phone – rang often as everyone called to enquire for R and his family, offer any help they could, give their very best wishes. After some time, while appreciating the good wishes and caring behind these calls, it also became clear that R was utterly exhausted – by his illness, by pain, by coping with the drugs he needed plus side effects, and also by the constant calls and visits, no matter how well-intended.

Discussion followed with the family and they agreed a plan. R's wife M would give frequent up-to-date news to their children and one or two close family members – who visited R for short spells (rather than extended visits) and then let everyone who enquired know how R was feeling. Rather than trying to phone or call at the house, friends, colleagues and neighbours then asked about R's health and progress by contacting one of his close relatives. Again, good communication and teamwork were the key to sharing the load and building the best possible all-round care.

A few family members, friends, neighbours and colleagues find they can't cope with even the thought of possibly difficult discussions and situations, and may make the decision, either consciously or unconsciously, to be less involved, or not involved at all. People without any personal experience of long-term home caring often have no idea, can't imagine – or don't want to imagine – what may be involved. Some people retreat and stay away because they feel helpless, or perhaps they fear not being able to cope. Still others have some idea of what the carer is coping with and are happy they are not in the same situation, happy not to be involved. Home carers' time and energy for social activities are rare, and new contacts become fewer and fewer.

Where to start? As noted earlier, local medical and social services, telephone and local community directories can be a good beginning. They won't have all the answers. Perhaps they've never been asked before – and your enquiry may spur them to find what you need, and then also help others in a similar situation.

Telephone helplines can be a great source of support; just being able to talk to someone who understands, be able to ask questions and express worries, is a comfort and relief. Volunteers often have personal experience of similar situations and have time to listen to your individual story, and they may be able to suggest other helpful contacts or direct you to another charity with more specialist knowledge of your loved one's condition.

Self-help groups exist literally to self-help – each other as well as themselves – through sharing experiences, sharing information, sharing whatever they can. If you're lucky you may find a good self-help group near you, although in a rural area 'local' may be a relative term...

How I found much-needed help in a rural area

Over many years I'd been part of all sorts of different groups, e.g. Brownies, Youth Club, Samaritans, music, drama, writing and choir groups. However, they were all well established before I joined, and they already had recognised patterns for meeting, for discussion and for making group decisions.

As outlined in the Introduction to this book, when my daughter told me of her diagnosis, I had no information at all beyond the names Anorexia and Bulimia, and not knowing the phrase 'eating disorder' was quite a handicap. *I don't have a problem, why do you keep on fussing!* was my daughter's reaction to any expression of concern about her skeletal appearance. I'd have given anything to find a self-help group or telephone helpline to give me information and some idea of how to help Jay.

In the meantime I kept searching for local support. In the absence of any information or support, and with no real clue as to how to find any helpful contacts, I kept on hoping that somewhere, somehow, a guardian angel might appear. Finally I asked if I could put up a small poster at the local library and at the GP surgery, giving my phone number and asking if anyone else had home experience with Anorexia and Bulimia. It was through that initial telephone link that I was contacted by a few others saying that they too were trying to cope with an eating disorder in their own families. This was the beginning of a small support group in north-east Scotland, initially with three other parents meeting occasionally in the back room of a pub in Keith, a central point and twenty miles from all of us. We shared what we could of our very different experiences, discovering there were many recognisable similarities too. The saying *'The blind leading the blind'* comes to mind! However, that mutual meeting and being able to talk with someone who could relate to what was happening at home was crucial in helping us all to cope.

One of this small group knew of the Eating Disorders Association (now beat-uk), and our group and small telephone link joined up with their national telephone helpline. Here we found people who could not only offer information about eating disorders, but who could also relate to the experiences of folk in our own group.

A few more months down the line we decided we'd like to meet in quieter surroundings, although still in that central location. Thanks to a suggestion from Dr Millar of Aberdeen Eating Disorders Department we found a room free in the local hospital where we could meet for two hours once a month on a Saturday afternoon (to allow for various work commitments – among our members as well as at the hospital). We discussed confidentiality within the group, membership and organisation; we agreed what we wanted and needed, what was realistic, and our first steps.

Through these discussions we worked out a format for our meetings – how to ensure everyone had time and space to talk about individual difficulties in their own situation, time to share and discuss any information – helpful or otherwise – that we'd come across. Literally, we were a self-help group.

Whether singing or drama, computers or sport, reading, upholstery, writing, golf or care giving at home, two heads are better than one, and a group – another kind of team? – is even better. Perhaps reading of these experiences in my community might offer some ideas of how you could seek support in your own very different situation.

Actively look for helpful contacts – even finding one other person can help to share the load.

What kind of contact, what kind of group?

Today there are lots of online groups with interests in common, lots of charities and other organisations large and small. Sometimes it feels good to be able to talk freely without revealing even your real name. However, real people making face-to-face contact, perhaps sharing a pot of tea or coffee while exploring new pathways and support, sharing personal experiences and discussing what helped them or not, is very different from a voice on the phone or words on a computer screen. In common with many others, at different times I have found them all helpful.

Check with your local health or medical centre, local paper, library and so on. Ask friends, neighbours and other local contacts. Does the group you're looking for already exist? If so, where do they meet and when? Work out how to get to the venue at the right time and then go and check it out. It may be exactly what you're looking for – great! But ... it may not.

On phone helplines you have the choice to give your name or not, or you can choose a different name to give. A bigger organisation may be able to put you in touch with someone living locally – again, worth a try.

Helpline volunteers are trained to respect confidentiality. I re-trained with EDA, and then, following training, committed two to three hours at a regular time every week. Calls came from the local area, from all over the UK, and even from much further away, including America and Germany. Some people (including volunteers) like to give a name, their own or a pseudonym, while others prefer not to. Again, I learned a lot about the huge variations in the disorders and in each home care experience.

Perhaps you might consider helping as a volunteer in this way and commit a few hours a week to taking calls?

You've decided to go ahead and establish a new group?

If possible, find out about and contact any relevant existing charities and groups, giving information about your group. Ask for advice and support, as well as leaflets to give out.

Organise an open meeting – how?

Identify a suitable venue, set a convenient date and time. Having decided on Keith as a central meeting point, our first meetings were in the quiet back room of a hotel – I simply went in one afternoon and asked the owner if it would be ok for us to meet one evening a week in the back room, and asked which was his quietest night. He made us very welcome.

Whatever your own situation, if you come across anyone sharing similar experiences, ask for any suggestion they have for ways forward. If they can, most people are glad to be able to help.

Later, our group joined forces with the Aberdeen self-help group NEEDS (North East Eating Disorders Support Scotland). Through them we heard about SEDIG (Scottish Eating Disorders Interest Group) – a group that meets at least twice a year, composed of a mix of professionals and home carers all with a common interest: to share relevant information, discussion, experiences and expertise. Later all of this led to our strong campaign to improve ED services in Scotland.

Beginnings

Publicise as much as possible – by word of mouth, by telephoning or emailing contacts, posters in health centres, surgeries, gyms, schools, the press...

Note – call charges can add up, especially in rural areas when phoning a distance, as can advertising in the press. Unless you can make posters yourselves, this will probably also cost money for printing etc. So consider how best to operate in *your* circumstances, and where any necessary funding will come from.

First meetings – a few initial ideas

Welcome. Introduce yourself and any others who've helped start the ball rolling. Explain why you feel it's a good idea to get together. Ask everyone to give their first name, say why they came along, what they are hoping for from the meeting. You could also lead a brief mention or discussion about confidentiality being necessary – or not.

Making brief notes of what is discussed, plus any decisions made, can be very useful later.

Discuss. *Does everyone agree that trying to organise regular support meetings is a good idea?* If not, no group! If yes, read the following and decide what is relevant to your own situation.

Who is willing to help with the organisation of a group – for instance, finding a suitable regular venue, making bookings? **Remember** to make a note of volunteers, and if decisions are made, note who is going to follow through on those decisions and how.

Who may attend meetings? A group decision – possible involvement of doctors and other professionals? Or only for home carers, with occasional speakers invited?

Any resources needed? Who might help with these?

Any basic rules? For instance, confidentiality regarding whatever is said at any meeting?

Date and time of next meeting? Any volunteers to help organise it?

Only so much can be covered in that initial meeting. Lots of other questions can be decided later. For instance:

Who will lead each meeting? The same person each time, or taking turns?

Frequency of meetings? E.g. once a month, once a week, or something else? What do members feel they need?

Possible speakers? Who could help the group, who would members like to meet?

Do we need a small 'Steering Group' to make decisions become reality? If so, what would they need to do, and how many volunteers are needed? (This would only apply if several people attend meetings.)

Anything else important when starting a group?

Depending on the individuals involved, every group will develop its own recognised and agreed rules. As always, there is no one size that fits all.

Also, in any group there will inevitably be all sorts of different views. Establishing a new group depends very much on individual contributions as well as open discussion and cooperation. However, a good support group can make all the difference to the lives of the people who are its members, and ultimately to those at the centre of all our caring efforts.

The group may be only two or three people living in a scattered community meeting up to share experiences and mutual support, or the family and close friends of a troubled individual, or possibly a much larger group of people in a wide area or in a city who all share personal experience – for instance, coping with Alzheimer's, schizophrenia, bipolar disorder, autism, or people struggling to beat a compulsive/ addictive condition ... or a myriad other conditions. In some cases people may be coping with more than one long-term condition.

Possibly, like NEEDS Scotland who meet one evening a month, you might find a mix of members – some who want to beat their health condition and appreciate the mutual support and encouragement of others, and some who are home carers.

A brief outline of a NEEDS Scotland meeting

- Everyone meets together at an agreed time.
- Welcome as above, including reminder at each meeting of the importance of confidentiality.
- Everyone there is invited to introduce themselves and say what they hope for from the meeting.
- A member who has previously agreed to do so will introduce the 'icebreaker' (see below).
- After the icebreaker, the group discusses the experiences and concerns that individual members want to share. Sometimes there may be a theme agreed in advance by group members to guide the discussion. Sometimes there may be an invited speaker.
- Anyone who doesn't wish to share a personal experience at that meeting simply says 'Pass'.
- Then the group breaks into two or perhaps more smaller groups for discussion: a group for people currently recovering from an eating disorder, and another for carers, each group with an experienced group member or 'facilitator' who has had personal experience either as a home carer or has had their own struggle with the disorder and has beaten it.

Facilitators are volunteers who, after prior discussion and agreement by the group, help to make sure that *everyone* has a chance to share their own personal difficulties with the group, describing what they find helpful and what they find difficult.

Discussion groups

Where a self-help group has members with different backgrounds and experiences, e.g. some home carers and some actively fighting the condition, and when numbers attending the meeting are larger than about ten, breaking into smaller groups for discussion can ensure that everyone has more time to share their experiences.

Icebreakers

Whatever the group, an *icebreaker* can be a very useful starting point for discussion. It can help to start a home team round-the-table get together and discussion, or a discussion with friends, or it may be used at the start of a more formal group meeting.

Some of the icebreakers can be helpful in individual relaxation as well as in a group situation.

Here are a few icebreakers from NEEDS Scotland meetings (with thanks to Carol, Pam, Heather, Margaret, Di and others):

Colours/feelings

A selection of different coloured pieces of paper are placed on the table and each person chooses two colours that reflect how they feel that day.
Discuss our choices and how we feel.

Trust/faith

Discuss what these words mean to us and how we experience them in our lives.

Festival

An open discussion of our hopes and fears leading up to Christmas, or another festival, and everything around it.

New Year

An open discussion at the start of the year, examining fresh starts, small steps, no pressure, possible resolutions. What do *you* hope for in the year ahead?

Looking forward

We all think about and focus on something we are looking forward to, then share our thoughts and how we feel about it.

Quotes and sayings

Share a quote or saying that really helped you, made you think, or simply made you smile. A few sayings friends have shared with me:

Don't be afraid of misfortune and do not yearn after happiness; the bitter doesn't last forever and the sweet never fills the cup to overflowing.

Solzhenitsyn

God grant me the serenity to accept the things I cannot change, the courage to change the things I can, and the wisdom to know the difference.

Reinhold Niebuhr

Life is not about waiting for the storms to pass – it's about learning to dance in the rain!

Vivian Greene

Make every day count – you don't know how many days you have, or how many other people have.

Unknown

What is your own favourite quote or saying?

Today

Discuss today. Something *good* that happened to you, that you saw, heard, said, felt – anything at all you found positive.

Objects

Bring a selection of different objects and ask everyone to choose one. Discuss our choices, why we chose them, why we like them. Write about our chosen objects.

I am, I can!

Give each person a sheet of paper and a pen and ask them to draw a small circle and write 'I am' in it. Then draw 'petals' around the circle. Write in each petal something that *'I am'* – e.g. a mother, son, daughter, sister, friend, uncle, auntie...
Do the same with *'I can'* – e.g. laugh, sing, walk, run, sing, hop, read, draw...
Share and enjoy the good feeling it brings.

The 'Crap Sandwich'

Give each person three small triangles of paper and a pen (or this can simply be a discussion).
On one triangle (the bottom slice), *write something good about today.*
On the next triangle (the nasty stuff in the middle), *write the worst thing that happened today.*
On the last triangle (the top slice), *write something else good about today, to put the 'crap' in perspective.*
Discuss how we can try to balance good and bad things that happen in a day, a week, a month.
The 'Crap Sandwich' can be used to start discussion, or in conversation giving personal feedback about unacceptable behaviour, as outlined in Chapter 6, *Communication.*

Holidays, travel

Discuss how we spent our holidays, whether far-flung and exotic or just relaxing at home, our hopes and dreams for future holidays, various aspects of travel.

Lighthouse

Share what inspires us, guides and shows us the way, keeps us going – intuition, gut feeling, insight, clarity, wisdom, hope, how other people cope... What ignites us, energises, awakens us? A smile, laughter, feeling strong, coping, moving forward?

Trying to relax

What helps us best to relax? Walking, watching films, singing and music or something else? Share and discuss.

In all these icebreakers the main idea is to openly share and discuss our thoughts, ideas, feelings about the topics. Another couple of ideas for you to try – alone, or perhaps share with other home team members, friends or self-help group:

The Magic Stone

On the beach or perhaps in your garden or on a woodland or country walk, carefully choose a smooth stone which feels good under your fingers.

Your chosen stone is thousands of years old. Keep your special stone in your pocket or in your purse or under your pillow. It may be kept safely in one place or carried with you.

Remember your stone whenever you need it. Hold the stone in your hand and breathe deeply. Gently rub the smooth surface of the stone with your thumb.

Continue to rub the stone with your thumb, and name your worries – or sadnesses, or frustrations – one at a time. With each one you name, think carefully about it.

Continue to rub for several minutes. Think of how long this magic stone has existed, how many worries it has seen come and go in its long life – as well as the love, warmth and joy it has seen.

Name each worry one by one and give it to your magic stone. As they are rubbed away, feel the love, warmth and joy the stone also holds.

When you have given all your worries to the stone, continue stroking the smooth surface for as long as you wish.

Remember *– today's hassles are tomorrow's history.*

I like to keep my smooth magic stone, which I found on a local beach, in my pocket. When I found one for a dear friend, she later told me she took it with her when she was in hospital for an operation and kept it under her pillow, held it when she felt in need of comfort.

Beating the stress bugs...

Find some modelling clay, or some of the foam used for floral arrangements – anything that can be shaped.

Cover a table or other work surface with newspaper. Put your modelling material on a flat surface and select your tools to use on it.

Imagine those horrid and unwelcome little Stress Bugs which have invaded your mind and body when you were concentrating on much more important matters.

Squeeze and squash the modelling material into the shape of those horrible bugs which are affecting your life. What do they look like? Grotty and gruesome? Defiant and dreadful? Sly and slimy? Snaky and sneaky?

What would you like to do to them? Shred them? Bash them, smash them to bits, or chop them up?

Use your imagination. Let it go really wild, come up with other alternatives – your models are no longer foam or clay, they have turned into those nasty bugs.

Keep thinking of those Stress Bugs and how you feel about them. They represent your very worst enemy and they are trying their best to destroy your peace of mind.

Nasty little things! How dare those bugs attack you, invade your life without invitation!

Work at it until you have reduced those bugs to mush. Keep working on them as long as you want to, think about how they look, how you are destroying them, mashing them, reducing them.

Now what are you going to do with them? Bury them deep? Tie them in a bag to dispose of in the rubbish? Or some other way of disposing of them?

Once you're satisfied they've gone, what now? Celebrate! If they come back, you'll be ready for them!

Quiet times

Sitting, breathing quietly and deeply, can also help. Time sitting with the cat purring on your lap, walking the dog, leaning against a tree, watching birds in a garden, or a sunset.

Years on, I learned about Ray Owen's 2011 book *Facing the Storm: Using CBT, Mindfulness and Acceptance to build resilience when your world's falling apart*,[1] which also offers many suggestions about how to cope when facing any of life's storms.

As can the final strategy I offer in this book. It was taught to me by a friend years ago and I've used it ever since. I understand there are variations of the same or similar in many parts of the world.

In the light

Sun, moon, star, candle, firelight – all give us light to warm us or show us a way forward.

Find a time when you won't be disturbed. Choose your own favourite special place to sit in peaceful surroundings; this could be outdoors in a garden, in a park, on a beach or a hillside, in a field. Or indoors, perhaps in your favourite chair by a window at home; at a friend's house; in a church. Anywhere and at any time you can find a quiet space.

You may choose a candle to light, watch the firelight, or enjoy a natural source of light from the moon or the stars (do not use the sun for this exercise). Make sure you are comfortable.

Look at and into the light. Feel it gently surrounding you, radiating warmth.

Be aware of the air passing through your nose as you breathe gently and regularly.

After a while, begin to count your breaths. *One – two – three – four – five – six.* Return to one and begin again.

Repeat this several times. If your thoughts begin to wander, just notice the thought and start counting at one again.

Continue breathing gently and regularly.

When you're ready, change the counting to –

In – out.

Deep – slow.

Calm – ease.

Rest – release.

In this moment – precious moment.

Again, repeat for some time, quietly and peacefully. As before, if your mind wanders, restart. *In – out. Deep – slow. Calm – ease. Rest – release. In this moment – precious moment.*

Focus your mind and heart and soul on the light you've chosen. Continue *in – out, deep – slow...* Think of the light surrounding you, radiating warmth and helping to heal your pain and your exhaustion.

Continue in the light, carry it with you in your mind, and return to your special place as often as you can.

Now, having talked with so many home carers and knowing how differently things could have turned out for my daughter and for me, I feel thankful every day.

I hope you find what you need to help you continue your home caring in your own situation.

Good luck, and my very best wishes on your journey.

Note

1 Owen, R. (2011) *Facing the Storm: Using CBT, mindfulness and acceptance to build resilience when your world is falling apart.* Routledge.

Useful contacts and websites

Assist UK *'is a resource for people searching for disability advice and disability equipment through a network of disability living centres.'*
Redbank House, 1 Portland Street, Manchester M1 3BE
Tel: 0161 238 8776
www.assist-uk.org

Benefit Enquiry Line
Warbreck House, Warbreck Hill Road, Blackpool FY2 0YE
Tel: 0800 882 200
www.direct.gov.uk/disabilitymoney

British Association for Counselling and Psychotherapy (BACP)
BACP House, 15 St Johns Business Park, Lutterworth LE17 4HB
Tel: 01455 833 300
www.bacp.co.uk

British Red Cross *'helps people in crisis, whoever and wherever they are.'*
44 Moorfield, London EC2Y 9AL
www.redcross.org.uk

Carers Direct *'Social care support and information online and via Carers Direct on freephone. Advice on choosing social care, how to fund care, carers' breaks...'*
PO Box 4338, Manchester M61 0BY
Tel: 0808 802 0202
www.nhs.uk/carersdirect

Carers UK *'Independent information and support for carers.'*
20 Great Dover Street, London SE1 4LX
Tel: 0808 808 7777
www.carersuk.org

Carers Scotland, part of Carers UK, offers an excellent booklet entitled *'Finding the balance – promoting positive health'*. As well as offering practical sections on Keeping well, Eating well and Sleeping Well, Caring for your back, Exercise, Good Emotional Health, Complementary Medicine and several others, the booklet also lists many useful books, telephone and website contacts for family carers – including, for instance, suggestions about online life-skills training.

Caritas Legal Limited *'specialising in the protection of vulnerable groups. Our mission statement is to deliver – Clear and Relevant Innovative Tailor made, Accessible Solutions. We regularly advise on a range of issues including: Guardianship Applications, Intervention Orders, Powers of Attorney, Advanced Healthcare Directives, Self-Directed Support and Paying for residential care.'*

ChildLine *'Help for children and young people.'*
Tel: 0800 1111

Citizens Advice Bureau *'offer free, confidential, impartial and independent advice from over 3500 locations.'*
Contact details for local office in your phone book.
www.citizensadvice.org.uk

Citizens Advice Scotland
www.cas.org.uk

Childhood Bereavement Network *'We support families and educate professionals when a baby or child of any age dies or is dying, or when a child faces bereavement.'*
8 Wakley Street, London EC1V 7QE
Tel: 020 7843 6309
Email: support@childbereavement.org.uk
www.childhoodbereavementnetwork.org.uk

Compassionate Friends *'Healing support for those grieving loss by suicide.'*
53 North Street, Bristol BS3 1EN
Tel: 0845 120 3785
www.tcf.org.uk

Cruse Bereavement Care *'is here to support you after the death of someone close.'*
PO Box 800, Richmond TW9 1RG
Tel: 0844 477 9400
Email: helpline@cruse.org.uk
www.crusebereavementcare.org.uk

Disability Alliance UK *'National charity aiming to relieve poverty and improve the living standards of disabled people.'*
Universal House, 88–94 Wentworth Street, London E1 7SA
Tel: 020 7247 8776
www.disabilityalliance.org

Equality and Human Rights Commission (EHRC) *'monitors human rights and protecting equality across nine areas, including disability.'*
Tel: England 0845 604 6610
Scotland 0845 604 5510
Wales 0845 604 8810
www.equalityhumanrights.com

Equality Commission Northern Ireland
Tel: 028 9089 0890
www.equalityni.org

Gamblers Anonymous *'Gamblers Anonymous is a fellowship of men and women who have joined together to do something about their own gambling problem and to help other compulsive gamblers do the same.'*
www.gamblersanonymous.org.uk

Gam-anon *'Compulsive gambling is recognised as an emotional illness. As husbands, wives, partners, siblings or friends, we know that living with this illness can prove a devastating experience.'*
www.gam-anon.org.uk

Hearing Voices Network *'A support group providing information, support and understanding to people who hear voices and those who support them.'*
Tel: 0114 271 8210
www.hearing-voices.org

Macmillan Cancer Information and Support *'Our centres offer free, confidential support to everyone.'*
www.macmillan.org.uk

Marie Curie Cancer Care offers home nursing support as well as hospice care and comprehensive advice for patients on a range of key issues, listening to carers' experiences looking after a loved one with a life-limiting illness. Marie Curie Helper volunteers are specially trained to offer companionship and emotional support.
www.mariecurie.org.uk

MIND *'We're here to make sure anyone with a mental health problem has somewhere to turn for advice and support.'*
Tel: 0845 766 0163
www.mind.org.uk

NHS24.com *'offers an online health library and information by telephone or website.'*
Tel: 0845 4 24 24 24
www.nhs24.com

National Society for Prevention of Cruelty to Children (NSPCC) *'Help for adults concerned about a child.'*
Tel: 0800 5000
www.nspcc.org.uk
Email help@nspcc.org. uk

National Institiute for Health and Care Excellence (NICE) *'Evidence-based guidelines on treatments.'*
www.nice.org.uk

North East Eating Disorders Support Scotland (NEEDS Scotland) aims to offer information, help and support in a safe, caring and confidential environment to anyone affected by eating disorders – sufferers, family and other carers.
www.needs-scotland.org

Quarriers *'provides care and support for people with a disability, epilepsy, and for young homeless people'.*
Tel: 01505 616000/612224

Relate *'offers advice, relationship counselling, sex therapy, workshops, mediation, support face-to-face, by phone and through the website.'*
Premier House, Carolina Court, Lakeside, Doncaster DN4 5RA
Tel: 0300 100 1234
www.relate.org.uk

Rethink Mental Illness – *'National mental health charity: information; services and a strong voice for everyone affected by mental illness – challenging attitudes and changing lives.'*
Tel: 0300 5000 927
www.rethink.org

SAMH – Scottish Association for Mental Health *'Talking is one of the first steps to better mental health.'*
SAMH Information Service, Brunswick House,
51 Wilson Street, Glasgow G1 1UZ
Tel: 0141 530 1000
Email: *enquire@samh.org.uk*

Samaritans *'We're here 24 hours a day, 365 days a year. If there's something troubling you, get in touch.'*
Chris, PO Box 9090, Stirling FK8 2SA
Tel: 08457 90 90 90
Email: jo@samaritans.org
www.samaritans.org

Scottish Government *'Finding the Care that is Right for You.'* Information for older people on: Care at home; Supported housing; Funding; Getting Care; Care Homes; Local resources.
Care Information Scotland
Tel: 08456 001 001
www.careinfoscotland.co.uk

Scottish Eating Disorder Interest Group (SEDIG) 'A *mixed group of professionals and home carers, meeting twice a year.'*
www.sedig.co.uk

Spina Bifida Association *'is dedicated to enhancing the lives of those with Spina Bifida and those whose lives have been touched by this challenging birth defect. Its tools are education, advocacy, research and service.'*
www.spinabifidaassociation.org.uk

Stresswatch Scotland offers information leaflets and self-help tapes.
Tel: 01563 574144
www.stresswatchscotland.org

Time To Change works closely with young people, schools and parents – *'Watch films, read blogs, download resources and find out how you can start talking to your children about mental health.'*
www.time-to-change.org.uk/parents

VSA (Voluntary Service Aberdeen) *'Do you look after a friend or relative? Who is looking after you? Connections, Choices and Changes. A six week course for carers.*
Meet with other carers to learn new skills, explore how to stay healthy and resilient, respond to challenges and develop the confidence to take more control.'
Tel: 01224 212 021
info@vsa.org.uk

Index